FINDLAY GLASS:
The Glass Tableware Manufacturers, 1886-1902

by

James Measell

and

Don E. Smith

with
James Houdeshell
Aleda Mazza
Virginia Motter

Paperbound I.S.B.N. #0-915410-25-7
Hardbound I.S.B.N. #0-915410-26-5

Additional copies may be ordered from:
ANTIQUE PUBLICATIONS, INC.
P.O. Box 655
Marietta, Ohio 45750

INTRODUCTION

Several years ago, my good friend Jim Houdeshell, a long-time Findlay resident and avid glass collector, asked me this question, "Do you think we could do for Findlay glass what you did for Greentown?" He was referring, of course, to *Greentown Glass* (1979), which was published by the Grand Rapids Public Museum. Jim's goal was clear: to produce a book-length, definitive account of the glass tableware made at Findlay by five important factories.

By late 1982, the project began to take shape. I reviewed all of the painstaking research completed by Don E. Smith over several decades when he was preparing his *Findlay Pattern Glass* (1970). Don had interviewed glass-workers, dug for fragments at the factory sites, and read the old newspapers and other documents. With the help of the Hancock Historical Museum Association, a grant from the L. Dale Dorney Trust Fund of The Cleveland Foundation was obtained. This provided funds to acquire microfilm of glass trade industry publications and to travel to the Library of Congress to examine resources there which were not otherwise available.

While I pushed ahead with the historical research, Virginia Motter prepared the first drafts of lists of "every item in every pattern" known to collectors of Findlay glass. Over the better part of two years, these lists were expanded and checked and re-checked. Aleda Mazza and Don E. Smith contributed their knowledge of Findlay glass (and their moral support!) to these listings, too. Several glass collectors in the Findlay area loaned articles to be photographed.

Fellow glass historian and author Bill Heacock helped us establish contact with Dave Richardson of Antique Publications. Bill also shared aspects of his research and allowed us to use some illustrations from his publications.

This project was not without pitfalls. A week in February, 1985 set aside for photographing Findlay glass brought the season's worst snow-ice-sleet storm to northwestern Ohio! Weekends planned for writing and proofreading disappeared when personal matters became too pressing. Nonetheless, writing this book and working with Don, Jim, Aleda and Virginia was a pleasure.

James Measell

Box 1052
Berkley, MI 48072

TABLE OF CONTENTS

Chapter One
GAS AND GLASS IN FINDLAY

During the last quarter of the nineteenth century, the glass tableware industry in the United States underwent both rapid expansion and profound changes. Before the history of Findlay's glass tableware factories can be fully understood, one must be aware of the conditions and developments in the industry during the two decades following the Civil War.

American glass manufacturers were primarily individual entrepreneurs, and competition among them was strong. During the Civil War, they organized themselves, albeit loosely, into a confederation known as the Flint and Lime Glass Manufacturers of the United States. The gentlemen who assembled at the annual meetings between 1862 and 1866 represented three geographic regions: New England, especially the Boston area; the East Coast firms, chiefly Brooklyn and Philadelphia; and the West, composed of factories at Pittsburgh, a few at Wheeling and others scattered throughout Ohio and other states.

In many ways, these enterprises were alike. Located near abundant fuel sources (wood or coal), they employed relatively small work forces of skilled men to blow glass into a variety of shapes for utilitarian and/or decorative purposes. Employees were generally well-compensated, but there was no national trade union of glassworkers, although some local organizations may have existed. Goblets sold for the high price of $3.50 per dozen, and a like number of tumblers brought $1.30 (by 1888, when most of the pressed ware plants at Findlay were operating, the prices had dropped to 40¢ and 37¢, respectively). Finished products were shipped by rail or water. The line between financial success and failure was a narrow one, and many of the firms which entered the industry during the 1850s and 1860s were but memories a decade or two later.

By about 1880, the epicenter of the American pressed glassware business was, without doubt, Pittsburgh. Indeed, Allegheny County was probably the heart of all three branches of the entire glass industry: window and plate glass; green glass bottles; and tableware and lamp chimneys. According to the *Tenth Census* (1880), forty-four of the nation's ninety-one tableware and chimney plants were in Pennsylvania, and Allegheny and Philadelphia Counties jointly accounted for nearly 6.7 million dollars of capital. The counties ranked first and second in value of output, also, totaling about $7.4 million. There were thirty tableware and chimney plants in Allegheny County alone, employing over 4,000 workers and producing 3.2 million dollars in products annually.

The reasons for Pittsburgh's prominence were three-fold: the general westward expansion of the nation after the Civil War; the availability of coal for fuel; and the ready access to transportation facilities, both water and rail. Essentially the same advantages were of benefit to Wheeling, West Virginia and to Belmont County, Ohio, encompassing Martins Ferry, Bridgeport and Bellaire. The glass manufacturers of these areas joined with their counterparts at Pittsburgh in 1874 to form the Western Flint and Lime

Glass Protective Association, the first regional trade group in the glass industry. The organization grew in number and in influence, and by 1887 it was the cornerstone of the first viable national trade association, the American Association of Flint and Lime Glass Manufacturers.

Although the city of Pittsburgh and the state of Pennsylvania continued to hold their respective number one positions in the glass industry, other cities and states made dramatic increases. Between 1870 and 1890, the ranks of Ohio's glass plants grew from nine to 67; from 1884 to 1890 alone thirty-five new firms were founded. More than a dozen of these were in or near Findlay. Several of these made window glass or bottles, and some made a specialty of lamp chimneys. Five produced glass tableware—the Columbia Glass Company; the Bellaire Goblet Company; the Dalzell, Gilmore and Leighton Company; the Model Flint Glass Company; and the Findlay Flint Glass Company. This book is their story.

Glass factories came to Findlay in the 1880s for one major reason: natural gas. An almost perfect fuel for glassmaking because of its cleanliness and efficiency, natural gas seemed to exist in endless quantities in Hancock County, Ohio, during the 1880s. Natural gas is a colorless, odorless, lighter than air gas which is composed chiefly of a hydrocarbon compound called methane (CH_4). Formed below the surface of the earth by the decomposition of organic vegetable matter, natural gas often migrates through porous rocks and may reach the surface of the earth unless trapped in pockets within reservoir rocks by non-porous rocks called caps or seat seals above the reservoirs. Over one thousand feet below the surface of Hancock County lies the Trenton limestone, a band of dolomitic limestone [chemically, $CaMg(CO_3)_2$] perhaps five to six hundred feet thick. This limestone should not be confused with the Niagra limestone [chemical formula $CaCO_3$], which is often found at or near the surface of Hancock and surrounding counties.

Today's petroleum geologists recognize that Hancock County lies along the Findlay arch, a Trenton limestone formation once rich in natural gas and, to some extent, oil deposits comprising the Lima-Indiana district. Natural gas and oil are frequently found together when drilling, and salt water may accompany either or both. Much of the natural gas used in Findlay during the 1880s was, apparently, reasonably "dry" (i.e., free from salt water and/or oil) and relatively "sweet" (i.e., low in hydrogen sulfide, H_2S, which has a strong, unpleasant odor).

The discovery of natural gas in Findlay attracted both statewide and national attention during the 1880s. The Ohio State Geologist, Dr. Edward Orton, studied many of the wells, and the Findlay gas field was a prominent subject within geological reports on Ohio issued between 1886 and 1903. Writers from leading national periodicals such as *Harper's* and *The American Magazine* visited Findlay to observe both the industrial growth and the flaming natural gas standpipes which attracted sightseers from miles around.

Some recognition must be given here to the gentleman who was responsible for the discovery and economic use of natural gas in Findlay, Dr. Charles Oesterlin. In his *Preliminary Report on Petroleum and Inflammable Gas,* issued in 1886, Dr. Edward Orton had this to say:

> The credit of the discovery of high-pressure gas in the Trenton limestone belongs largely to one man, Dr. Charles Oesterlin, and old and highly respected citizen of Findlay. . . . Dr. Oesterlin seems to have been the only one who recognized that there was a source of light and heat . . . that could possibly be utilized in a large way. He urged, many years ago, the formation of a company to drill for gas. . . .

Other sources, such as Z. L. White's article in The *American Magazine* (December, 1887), paint a somewhat different picture of Oesterlin. Apparently the young German physician practiced homopathic (natural) healing, and this curiosity, combined with his penchant for approaching Findlay's businessmen with schemes for developing and using "nature gas," led to Oesterlin's reputation as "a crank." Although a company (the Findlay Gas Light Co.) had been formed by others to manufacture fuel gas from coal, Dr. Oesterlin was unable to gain financial support for his natural gas drilling projects unti some time in 1884.

By the early 1880s, of course, natural gas was being used in such manufacturing centers as Pittsburgh, especially in the iron and glass industries. Difficulties were encountered when the gas pressure dropped in cold weather or when oil and/or salt water filled the wells, but natural gas was clearly the fuel of the future. The Rochester Tumbler Company, about 30 miles from Pittsburgh, was operating solely on natural gas by 1880, and the glass trade journals were quick to sense the favorable economic impact of the fuel. The glass factories in and around Wheeling began to change over from coal to natural gas, even though this meant piping the natural gas from fields near Washington, Pennsylvania, about 25 miles away.

The weekly issues of *Crockery and Glass Journal* during 1886 are replete with news and comment concerning the use of natural gas in Ohio Valley glass factories. A column in the March 11, 1886, issue, for instance, described the manufacturers in Bellaire as "elated at the prospects of having natural gas for fuel . . . in the fall." By late that summer, natural gas was an established fact. The city of Wheeling held a celebration "larger than the centennial year," and 15,000 people turned out to view flaming natural gas from large escape pipes and hear a speech by Charles W. Brockunier, owner of a large glass plant and other interests. The September 9, 1886, issue of *Crockery and Glass Journal* reported his remarks, among which was the observation that Wheeling would have lost its glass factories if not for the coming of natural gas.

When drilling for natural gas had spread to Ohio's interior in the early 1880s, the publicity associated with a project in Bucyrus caught the attention of Dr. Charles Oesterlin. According to Orton, Dr. Oesterlin corresponded with the firm drilling at Bucyrus (the Gillespie Tool Company of Pittsburgh) and was soon able to interest

Charles Eckels (or Echols) and Henry Porch, both of Findlay, in forming a corporation and commencing explorations for natural gas. The threesome attracted a few more investors, and the Findlay Natural Gas Company was born.

Orton reports that drilling began "about October 20th [1884] on the east side of Eagle Creek [Lye Creek], and just beyond the corporation limits." A few weeks later, the drill struck natural gas; Orton describes the result: "The gas was lighted and the blaze shot up 20 or 30 feet above the standpipe. The light could be seen for 10 or 15 miles away, on all sides. Great excitement was naturally caused by the discovery, the people flocked into Findlay by the thousands to see the strange spectacle."

The discovery of natural gas at Findlay led to a great rush of drilling activity in Hancock County particularly, as well in northwestern Ohio and eastern Indiana generally. By April, 1886, there were seventeen more gas wells in the Findlay field and only one was a disappointment, yielding oil rather than natural gas. The major success was the Karg well, which, for those who enjoy putting superstition to rest, was the thirteenth gas well drilled in Hancock County, Oesterlin's, of course, being the first. The Karg well was on the south side of the Blanchard River near Liberty Street, just a few blocks from the busiest portions of town and close to a railway station.

The Karg well

Orton wrote that the roar of the well could be heard for two or three miles and the light from the flame seen for thirty-five or forty miles. When writing his *Brief History of Gas and Oil in Findlay* about 1940, Humphrey asserted that "the roar of this well was clearly heard for a distance of five or six miles, while the light was so intense that newspapers could be read at a distance of from nine to sixteen miles from the well." A reporter from Toledo, who visited Findlay in February, 1886, described the Karg as follows:

> Five or six miles before reaching Findlay a brilliant light is seen in the heavens, and a mile or two further on discloses to the vision a great cloud of fire. This was the great Karg well. Its proportions, intensity, and grandeur, increase as the town is neared, when church steeples and housetops are brought out with the distinctiveness of day. Unexplained, the phenomena would be awful and fearful. Passing into the main street of the town, the light from the burning Karg well is somewhat modified by the bright flames from the immense jets of gas shooting upward from the tops of the lamp posts. These jets are three or four feet in height and, under their flare, a pin in the street, which is one hundred feet wide, can be readily picked up, the finest print can be read as easily as in a parlor in Toledo lighted by the best gas one company can produce. It is impossible to give a correct idea of the impression made upon a stranger as he stands in the center of this wide, level street with long vistas of light north and south of him; the house fronts are as clearly defined as if the being of day were pouring the noon-day light upon them, and pedestrians on the street readily recognized blocks away. The effect was peculiar and inspiring.
>
> To obey the impulse to visit the monster who was shedding a light which, to unused eyes, exceeded anything before imagined, beyond the sun itself, a carriage was called and with the artist from the *Bee* we drove at once to it, more than a half mile from the hotel. As we neared the spot, sounds like the rustling waters of a great fall struck the ear, and in the houses where the windows looked in that direction, the interior was as light as day. Passing through several streets, the hack brought up suddenly one hundred feet from the well. The sounds of escaping gas from the standpipe now forcibly reminded me of Niagra, and as I looked up at the great cloud of flame shooting upward as if angry that there was not something for it to destroy, the feeling of the sublime called up by the great cataract forced itself still stronger upon me.
>
> The scene is one of indescribable grandeur. The well is located on the south bank of the Blanchard, which passes through the north part of town. It is 1,144 feet from the surface to the gas-bearing rock below, and the hole is five and five-eighths inches in diameter.
>
> As far as the eye has uninterrupted scope, the landscape is illuminated by this monster light, and persons could be distinctly seen more than half a mile away, and the color of their clothing readily discerned. Within a few hundred feet of the flame, with the cold, crisp atmosphere outside, it was uncomfortably hot. On the opposite side of the river, and for a considerable distance all about the well, the grass was growing with the luxuriance of May, and the water in the river below, everywhere else covered with ice, was blue and limpid as a lake.

The economic and social impacts of the discovery of natural gas in apparently dependable supply were soon felt in Findlay. Writing in 1886, Orton made these observations and predictions:

> The development of manufacturing industries at this point is without precedent in the history of Ohio towns. The population of Findlay has been more than doubled within the last year and will be doubled yet again in 1887, and the price of real estate has been multiplied, it is safe to say, if present rates are any gauge, many times; and for the last few weeks a strong current of speculative excitement has been sweeping through the entire region. Capitalists are gathering in from all quarters, and investments are being made in a very large scale, and it is certain that the developments of the last year will be found to be insignificant in comparison with what 1887 will have to show.

Little more than a year later, in his first full *Report of the Geological Survey of Ohio,* State Geologist Orton devoted a few pages to recounting the manufacturing interests which had come to Findlay: the Briggs Tool Works, where natural gas was used to weld iron and steel for the first time on June 8, 1886; seven glass factories, three in operation and four under construction; two iron rolling mills and a nail works; and an assortment of other firms making pressed bricks, furniture or other products. His remarks about the euphoria of 1887 are well worth quoting in full:

> The opening weeks of 1887 witnessed the breaking out of a speculative excitement of extraordinary intensity. The entire community was affected by it, nor was it confined even to the limits of the state. It found the city of Findlay, as already stated, with territorial limits of four square miles. It left it with twenty-four square miles on paper, the entire township having been brought into the city. A considerable part of the farm lands adjoining the town has already been broken up into "additions," and many of the latter are already divided into town lots. Streets are graded and shade-trees set. Several of the manufacturing establishments . . . are located in these additions, from two to three miles distant from the court-house.
>
> Within the present limits of the city it is estimated that seven hundred dwellings have already been built during 1887, and as many more are under contract to be completed before the end of the year. It is claimed that twice as many new

houses would be occupied this year, if they could be provided.

A local census taken in the spring of 1887, showed 10,221 persons residing within the four square miles that constituted the old town. This number has already been largely increased within these limits, and still further, by the establishment of the several additions above named. Estimates vary between 13,000 and 18,000 as to the number in Findlay in August, 1887.

Under the excitement of the first three months of 1887, the prices of real estate advanced to very extravagant figures. At the end of that time purchasers had disappeared and sales were thus arrested. A large number of important enterprises have, however, been established in the town since that date, attracted by grants of land, the offer of free fuel, and in some cases by stock subscriptions, aided by great effort and activity on the part of the Chamber of Commerce.

One class of population has reaped a rich harvest from the increase of prices of real estate, viz., the farmers who held the outlying lands around Findlay. They have received for their lands twice, three times, or even five times the prices at which they held them in 1886. Most of them were sagacious enough to take the tide as it rose. Comparatively little of the farming land of Findlay township remains in the hands of its old owners.

The efforts of developers and businessmen, acting in groups called syndicates or in formal organizations such as the Chamber of Commerce, must not go without notice here, for the inducements offered to manufacturers for locating their plants at Findlay were typical of the natural gas boom towns elsewhere in Ohio and, somewhat later, in Indiana. The plans and contracts were made in good faith, of course, but the future was not always to be as positive as some manufacturers and businessmen had hoped. At times, the needs of the citizens conflicted with those of the manufacturers, and the city found itself in the difficult position of providing for both orderly and equitable economic development in an often emotionally charged atmosphere.

The Columbia Glass Company first appears in the public records of Hancock County on May 25, 1886, when its proprietors signed an agreement with the Findlay Gas Light Company, which by this time, had been taken over by Dr. Charles Oesterlin and his fellow investors. The agreement, which was not officially recorded until November, 1887, allowed Oesterlin's group to drill a gas well on the Columbia's land. The glass factory would be charged $400 per year for natural gas to supply its furnaces, but, if the well produced a great flow of natural gas, the yearly fee would drop to $200. The amounts stated were to be firm for five years.

Three other glass tableware firms—the Bellaire Goblet Company; the Dalzell, Gilmore and Leighton Company; and the Model Flint Glass Company—had somewhat similar arrangements. When the Bellaire Goblet Company decided to relocate in Findlay from Bellaire, Ohio, a Findlay

The Gas Boom of 1887, taken at Crawford St. looking north.

NATURAL GAS ILLUMINATION. THE FIRST ANNIVERSARY OF THE APPLICATION OF NATURAL GAS TO THE MECHANICAL ARTS IN FINDLAY, O. JUNE 8TH, 9TH, AND 10TH, 1887.
PHOTOGRAPHED BY CROZIER & LINAWEAVER, OLD WHITE CORNER, FINDLAY, O.

newpaper cited the town's "unrivalled inducements of free sites and free fuel" as key factors in the firm's decision. A few days later, the same newspaper lauded the Howard and Swing syndicates for their "generous donations of land and money." A free natural gas well was to be provided for the Bellaire; later, after the plant was rebuilt following a fire in 1889, the Bellaire signed a contract with the City of Findlay Gas Trustees for natural gas at $400 per year. The Model Flint Glass Company, a smaller concern, paid $100 per year for its natural gas.

The Harper land syndicate and four other similar groups apparently agreed to pay the Dalzell, Gilmore and Leighton Company a bonus of as much as $15,000 to move their factory from Wellsburg, West Virginia, to Findlay. The guarantee provided for $10,000 to be paid within a month after glassmaking commenced, and further payments of $2,500 each to be made when employment levels reached 250 and 300. Some difficulties arose, and the Dalzell, Gilmore and Leighton Company sued the syndicates, winning a judgment of $4,971.63 in late 1890, all of which was reported in *Crockery and Glass Journal* for December 4, 1890. The final resolution of the case may have taken some time, however, for a Findlay newspaper reported on February 19, 1894, that the case was to be heard in Superior Court at Cincinnati.

As one might expect, the offers of free land, free or nearly free natural gas and the payments of cash bonuses — all of which were not unusual in the Ohio and Indiana natural gas boom towns — were sometimes born of a spirit of optimism which outdistanced the resources at hand. Nevertheless, the 1886-1889 period was a time in which Findlay's hopes were matched by its realizations. The glass tableware plants flourished, and the town prospered from the influx of population and increases in land values.

Success in some quarters very often brings about resentment in others, and the city of Pittsburgh was clearly threatened by a loss of manufacturing industries, particularly glass factories. A note from Pittsburgh in the February 24, 1887, issue of *Crockery and Glass Journal* is somewhat defensive and petulant in tone, but the feelings expressed and the conditions described are revealing:

The natural gas boom has departed from this city and located itself apparently in northwestern Ohio, where all kinds of inducements are offered to glass manufacturers to plant themselves, including houses and lands, free gas, freedom from taxation, immunity from strikes, good water and innumerable other benefits not elsewhere obtainable. However, as rival towns out there are injudiciously belittling one another's ability to furnish the facilities promised, and are otherwise making indiscreet exposures of one another's weak points, the movement of capital thither has not been such as can be considered a generous recognition of the persuasive influences employed.

In June, 1887, Findlay applauded its good fortune in a

three day pageant dubbed the "First Annual Celebration of the Application of Natural Gas to Mechanical Arts." Fifty years later in 1937, Findlay paused to recall this event; a book produced from those recollections, William D. Humphrey's *Brief History of Gas and Oil in Findlay,* offers such a full report of the 1887 event that it bears repeating here:

Never again can the three days of June 8, 9, 10, 1887, be duplicated, either in scope, details, decorations or spirit. Celebrations may come, and celebrations may go, but that of Findlay fifty years ago will remain above and apart from all others. This can be stated without undue exaggeration, simply because the conditions and surroundings of Findlay made it true.

It was a high point in a year that was filled with high hopes; the land boom, industrial growth, undiminished reserves of natural gas, unusual crowds, all added to give flavor and point to the great celebration of natural gas.

Thus, we turn back the pages of history to the dawn of a beautiful, warm, sunny June day—the eighth of June, 1887. The weather was ideal, although a bit sultry. The early morning trains arrived loaded with sightseers, and at nine o'clock the streets were filled with a laughing, jostling, noisy crowd moving to and fro under the great arches, fifty-eight in number which spanned the streets from Lincoln to the bridge over the Blanchard to the north. At Sandusky Street the arches crossed from opposite corners, meeting at the center, and were decorated with evergreens and lights. Here and there a banner stretched between arches called attention to the fact that:

"Industrial Arts Lead to a More General Diffusion of Knowledge"

"It Costs $1.05 To Keep Warm"

"Varied Industries Multiply the Blessings of Life"

"Thirty-one Factories Located Within One Year"

Elsewhere a banner noted that one might consider:

"Findlay, the Center of the World"

However, none indicated great progress in labor saving for women than the one which proudly announced that:

"Women Split No Wood In Findlay"

The implications of this last one prefers not to follow up too closely.

On the side residential streets and beyond the business section, visitors had an opportunity to marvel at the decorations on the private homes of Findlay. As a reporter of the occasion says:

"Nearly every residence in the city, at least the majority of those on the principal streets, had some decorations, and in many cases they were lavish and beautiful beyond anything ever seen in Findlay. Not only were flags, buntings, evergreens, flowers and mottoes used with good effect, but the gas torch and jet, the latter encircled with globes of various tints and colors, were brought into requisition." It might be added that in many instances these burned day and night.

The order of events for the day included the laying of cornerstones for factories in West Findlay—"our promising suburb in the southwest"; a military drill on the Fair Grounds in the afternoon; and the grand illumination and official ceremonies at the Wigwam in the evening.

At 9:30 A.M. the procession formed at the corner of Main and Front Streets, marching from that point down Front Street to the Lake Erie and Western Railroad where special trains awaited to carry the marchers to West Findlay. Included in this procession were the Findlay and Forest Cantons, the Marion, Indiana, and Muncie, Indiana Cantons, Patriarch Militant (the military order of the Independent Order of Odd Fellows), the Northwestern and Northside Bands, and citizens. The Patriarch Militants were in official charge of the ceremonies of the morning, which included laying the cornerstones for the LaGrange Rolling Mills, Moore Chair Factory, and the Findlay Door and Sash Factory. Formal ceremonies in charge of Past Grand Master F. B. Zay were held at the site of the LaGrange Mill; the principal address was given by Past Grand Master Jacob F. Burket.

With the conclusion of these ceremonies the organizations returned to the city. At 1:30 the procession was re-formed and marched south on Main Street to the Fair Grounds between Jeffras Avenue and the railroad. Here a drill, military in character, was held. Only two Cantons of the Patriarch Militants took part, those from Marion and Muncie, Indiana. The prizes offered were $750 and $250, first and second prize, respectively. Following the drill, a fair crowd remained to witness a ball game between the Rosenthals, a local team, and the Tiffins.

The climax of the day came when with the approach of darkness, the torches and lights on the arches on Main Street were touched off and showed up with grand effect. Nothing like it was ever seen before, and exclamations of astonishment and wonder were to be heard on every hand. The arches over the tramway leading from the Main Street bridge were a sea of fire. The Chamber of Commerce building (located on the northwest corner of Main and West Front, now the Cusac Block) was surrounded by a line of colored lights, and the bridge was most attractively filled with designs of a similar character.

Of the arches over Main Street, the circular rim contained gas jets, while the uprights were decorated with jets enclosed in vari-colored globes. How overwhelming the effect must have been can only be imagined.

Impressive to the sight was the spectacular

waste of gas in a manner which in the end contributed to defeat the very object it was meant to obtain.

Overlapping the events at the Fair Grounds was a reception held for Senator Sherman in the Presbyterian Church at 5:30 P.M. Mr. Wilson Vance presided and introduced the Senator, who responded in a brief speech in which among other things he confessed that he had no conception of the greatness of our natural gas field which he termed "one of the marvels in history which grow greater as the ages roll on."

Following Mr. Sherman, General C. H. Grosvenor and former Govenor Foster made brief addresses. The audience then broke up into an informal reception.

Thursday evening saw Findlay's streets crowded to capacity. At 8:30 a procession again formed and moved north to the Wigwam where a banquet for a thousand persons was prepared, and where as many more had seats for the speeches and the ball which were to climax the day. Among the distin-

guished guests present were Senator Sherman, Governor Foraker, Chief Justice Waite, Judge Welker of the United States Court, the Honorable Samuel Young, Professor I. N. Vail of Barnesville, Ohio, Professor Edward Orton, State Geologist, Murat Halstead, the great editor from Cincinnati, and a host of others, including the Honorable E. R. Kennedy, M. C., the Honorable George Seeny, M. C., Ex-Governor Foster, and I. E. Dean ("Farmer" Dean, of Lima).

Following the call to the banquet, Reverend J. R. Mitchell gave the invocation, after which the guests were seated at large tables and a well-prepared course banquet was served, with plenty of champagne. Dr. Anson Hurd acted as toast-master.

Space will not permit a detailed account of all the responses which were made in the following order:—

"Causes, Sources, and Permanency of Natural Gas"
    —responded to by Professor I. N. Vail.

"Gas As Applied To Mechanical Arts"—
responded to by Professor Edward Orton,
State Geologist.

"President of the United States"—responded to by
Honorable E. R. Kennedy, M. C.

"Congress of the United States"—responded to by
Honorable George Seeny, M. C.

"Petroleum, Ohio Holds a World's Supply"—
responded to by "Farmer" Dean.

"Industrial Developments in the United States"—
responded to by the Honorable John Sherman.

"The Future of the American People"—responded
to by Edward Everett Hale.

"Labor and Capital in Their Relationship"—
responded to by Murat Halstead.

"The Ladies"—responded to by L. L. Morey.

"The Ever Watchful Guardians of the People's
Interest, Honorable Mayor and City Council"—
responded to by J. R. Kagy.

The scope and breadth of the above program of
toasts need hardly be commented upon, and, as a
poetic reporter might have written, dawn was pierc-
ing the veil of night ere it ended.

Two hundred guns awakened the citizens, as
perchance were asleep, to Friday, the final day of
the celebration. Like its predecessor, the day was
forbidding, being cool and cloudy. Ardor was not
dampened, however, and by 9:30 the streets were
once again being filled rapidly. Music from thirteen
bands stimulated and enlivened the milling crowds
which increased with each new train. At 10:00
o'clock the T. & O. C. train arrived from Toledo
with twelve coaches crowded to capacity, four of
the coaches being occupied by the Toledo Cadets
and Toledo visitors, the others filled with visitors
from Indiana. At noon a great trainload arrived by
way of the Lake Erie and Western, fifteen coaches
in all, unloading some 2,000 additional visitors.
The Jeffersonian states: "It is safe to say 20,000
people were present."

Friday was given over to military events in the
morning, and a Grand Parade and Band competition at the Wigwam in the evening.

At 11:30 A.M. the procession got under way
for Camp Garfield where the military competition
was to be held. Represented in this drill were the
crack military company of Toledo, the Toledo
Cadets; Battery B, Gatling Gun Squad of Cincinnati; the Columbus Cadets from the State University; the Wooster City Guards; the Geneva Rifles,
Geneva, Ohio; and the Lima Military Company.

The procession itself was made up in the following order:

Colonel Thorpe and Staff
Northwestern Band, Findlay
Kenton and Ada Regimental Bands
Toledo Cadets
Willie Boos Band, Tiffin

Battery B, Gatling Gun Squad
Ligonier Band, Ligonier, Indiana
Big Six Band, Springfield, Ohio
Wooster City Guards, Wooster, Ohio
Little Six and Octette Bands, Upper Sandusky
Co. 9, 5th Regiment, Ohio National Guards
Eldorado Band
Co. H., Sec. Regiment, Ohio National Guards
Leipsic Band
Geneva Rifles, Geneva, Ohio
Bloomdale Band
Lima Military Company
K. of P. Band, Cleveland
Findlay Military Company
Bluffton Boys' Band

The competitive drills began at 2:00 o'clock.
The judges of this event gave the Toledo Cadets
first prize of $1,000; the Columbus Cadets, second,
$500; and the Wooster Guards, third, $250.

Late in the afternoon a large audience gathered
at the Wigwam where Colonel James A. Bope
delivered an address on "Art, Music and Literature."
Following this, Honorable Jacob F. Burket extended
Findlay's invitation to a band concert open to the
world in the evening.

Later in the evening, a large audience assembled
at the Wigwam for the formal ceremonies opening
the celebration. The so-called Wigwam derived its
name from its general architectural style. It was
built on a portion of ground which was later to be
the old Athletic Park, lying between East Front
Street and the river. The site has been completely
destroyed by changes in the river channel.

Music for the ceremony was furnished by the
Findlay Glee Club; the official address of welcome
was delivered by Mr. E. T. Dunn. Following Mr.
Dunn, General A. P. Kennedy of Bellefontaine and
General D. W. Day both spoke, after which the
assemblage broke up.

Boom! Boom! Boom! One hundred guns at
sunrise awakened Findlay to the second day of the
celebration. Thursday opened inauspiciously as to
weather, with a dark and gloomy morning following
a night of rain. To many the outlook was anything
but encouraging, but as the trains began to arrive
and the rain held off, doubts were dispelled. The
Jeffersonian reported that "there were scarcely less
than 25,000 people present for the second day."
Each incoming train brought crowds, together with
the various lodges of the Knights of Pythias, who
were to have charge of the main events of the day.
During the morning, Senator Sherman and his
party arrived and were escorted to the home of
Wilson Vance, president of the Chamber of Commerce, where the Senator was to be the guest of
the Vance family.

On the streets the milling throngs were amused
and interested by the marching and countermarch-
ing of the visiting bands and lodges. The official

9

program called for a repetition of Wednesday's procedure of laying cornerstones. This time they wre to be laid in the northeast section of the city and included those of the Briggs Iron Mill, the Carrothers Rolling Mill and the Findlay Window Glass Company. These ceremonies were to be in chage of the Knights of Pythias. As before, a special train was held at the Lake Erie and Western Railroad for the participants, but for some unknown reason, this part of the program was not carried through on time. It was eleven o'clock when the procession actually formed in the following order:

Findlay Lodge, K. of P. Band, Cleveland
Red Cross Division, No. 22, Toledo
Miami Division, No. 35, Toledo
Springfield Band
Champion City Division, No. 44, Cleveland
Willie Boos Band, Tiffin
Pickway Division, No. 30, Tiffin
Eldorado Band
U. S. Grant Division, No. 32, Leipsic
Boys' Band of Bluffton

The procession moved north on Main Street, then northeast on the Lake Erie and Western Railroad to the Findlay Window Glass Company on Walnut and Blanchard, where a new building was to be erected. Official ceremonies were in charge of Grand Chancellor S. A. Court, of the State Lodge, Knights of Pythias. At the close of the ceremony the procession returned to the city. The cornerstone of the Carrothers Rolling Mill was later laid by a committee. The record of this day does not state what, if anything, was done about the Briggs Iron Mill.

Early in the afternoon the procession re-formed and moved south on Main Street to Maddox Avenue, now Lima Avenue, to the site of the Ohio Lantern Company, then located where the Cooper Tire Plant now stands. After appropriate ceremonies at this point, the parade continued to the Fair Grounds where a drill of the Divisions was held before a large crowd of people. The Findlay Daily Republican reports the event as follows:

"The maneuvering altogether was excellent and round after round of applause greeted the boys as they executed the fine movement of the drill. The Red Cross Division of Cleveland came first and won many friends. They were followed by the Springfield Division, the Pickway Division of Tiffin, and the Toledo Division, all of whom showed good records, and won cheers and applause from the audience."

The prizes offered for the competition were $500 for the best division, $250 for the second, and $100 for the third.

Due to the lateness of the hour, the ball game scheduled to follow the drill was postponed, and the procession re-formed and marched back to the center of the city.

Friday evening witnessed the climax of the celebration in another great parade which included:

Colonel Freeman Thorpe and Staff
Mayor and City Council
Findlay and Ligonier Band
Colored Odd Fellows
Distinguished Guests in Carriages
Chief, Fire Department
Willie Boos Band
Steamer No. 1 and Hose Cart
North Side Band
North Side Engine and Carts
Juvenile Hose Company
Eldorado Band
Little Six Band
Findlay, Canton Patriarch Militant
Octette Band
Toledo Cadets
Wooster City Guards
Lima Military Company
Columbus Cadets
Bluffton Boys' Band

After watching the spectacle, a reporter for the Toledo News Bee wrote thus:

"From the streamers, hand engine, and hook and ladder trucks were constantly discharged fireworks which made the scene beautiful to look upon. Many thousand people viewed the parade, and Main Street with its torches, globes, fireworks and moving companies, as well as the thousands of people presented a most striking scene. It is estimated that 30,000 strangers walked the path of light last night."

As for the band contest, prizes were offered for the largest band and for the band coming the greatest distance; in addition, there were three prizes for bands falling in the rating of first class, second class and third class. The winners of these various awards were:

First Class — Boos Band, Tiffin, first prize, $500; Ligonier Band, second prize, $300.

Second Class — Big Six, first prize, $300; Little Big Six, second prize, $200; K. of P., Cleveland, third prize, $150.

Third Class — Octette, Upper Sandusky, first prize, $125; Sec. Reg. O.N.G., second prize, $75; Bloomdale, third prize, $50.

Largest Band — Boos' Band, first prize, $500.

Band Coming Greatest Distance, Ligonier Band, Ligonier, Indiana, $500.

On Saturday morning the last event of the celebration was held, whether it was an afterthought or missed its scheduled place in the program cannot be said. This was a Gatling Gun exhibition by the famous Company B, Gatling Gun Squad of Cincinnati. As the rat-t-t-t died away the great celebration of the application of natural gas to the mechanical arts passed into history, but many now living who witnessed it testify to the fact that nothing like it was ever seen before or since in their opinions. Spectacular, exciting, noisy and vibrant, it was but a fitting expression to the fever of the day. Conceived on a large scale, aimed at those beyond its confines, it dramatized Findlay and natural gas as nothing else could have done.

What industrialist could fail to be appreciative of the great store of cheap fuel as he viewed the torches and jets buring day and night; when he saw with his own eyes the wells; when he listened to the optimistic expressions on all sides; what worker could fail but to rejoice in a community which could offer him work, and in addition fuel for heat and cooking, and a source of light, at a price which seemed next to nothing.

One and all were impressed, and the record of the years of 1887 and 1888 and 1889 show that Findlay had sold itself. It was a great show, that celebration of fifty years ago.

The celebration brought attention to Findlay from all quarters. An article appeared in the *New York Herald* on June 11, 1887. The national periodicals in the glass industry — *Pottery and Glassware Reporter* and *Crockery and Glass Journal* — made mention of the event, of course. Among the most interesting accounts in an Ohio publication is that of the *Illustrated Graphic News;* the June 18, 1887 issue featured a full page sketch on the cover plus five pages inside, including a two-page montage entitled "Four Great Days in the History of Findlay, O., The Gas Centre of the World" and portraits of seven prominent citizens.

In August, 1887, D. C. Connell of Findlay published a small "souvenir Album" of the city. A number of interesting photos of city landmarks were included, and the written text lauded Findlay as "the only city in the world having 60,000,000 cubic feet of gas per day, equal to 3,260,000 pounds of coal, which is furnished free as the air to every manufacturer who settles within her borders." Similar sentiment pervades the large, attractive volume *Findlay Illustrated,* which was issued in 1889:

> The City has become in a measure a kind of Mecca, and men journey from long distances to view its wonders, even as the Queen of Sheba visited Jerusalem to behold the wonders of the temple and harken to the wisdom of Solomon. Everything looks so new and is so expensive, the evidence of thrift is so apparent on every hand, that the stranger imagines it to be a city of yesterday, with a growth as rapid and a development as sudden as the magical cities of the farther west.

Elsewhere in the book, the City of Findlay's Gas Trustees expressed their faith that the great flow of natural gas would last "for several centuries."

Given the boundless optimism and the contagious enthusiasm expressed in the quotations above, it may be difficult to come to grips with the historical realities of Findlay's relatively short-lived affair with natural gas. The facts are these: from the onset, natural gas development was characterized by conflicts between private companies and, eventually, with the City of Findlay itself; the supply of natural gas began to peter out, and by the early 1890s, some of the glass factories left Findlay to relocate; agreements made between land syndicates and manufacturing interests could not be kept and lawsuits resulted.

To today's reader, accustomed to public utilities and municipal plants, Findlay's situation in the mid-1880s may be hard to believe. When the Oesterlin gas well proved successful, those who had invested in it sought to maximize their profits by piping the flow to various points for domestic and commercial use. Other drillers soon struck natural gas too, of course, and they vied with one another for customers. A major confrontation was between Oesterlin's group and a rival concern which had been formed some years earlier with the intention of manufacturing artificial gas from coal, a well-known but relatively expensive process. The Karg well was in the hands of the latter group, and, gradually, the Findlay Gas Light Company grew in financial strength. In the early months of 1885, the competition must have been especially interesting, as the two firms laid gas mains virtually side by side in Findlay's streets. Oesterlin's fellow investors sold their interests soon thereafter, and a single private company, known apparently as the Findlay Gas Light Company, emerged.

By today's standards, the natural gas rates charged to Findlayites are almost impossible to imagine. Cooking stoves were supplied at $1.00 per month, and house lights were 15 to 30¢ per month. Even a big boiler in a manufacturing plant cost only $150-200 per year! There were no gas meters as there are today; customers were charged flat fees for the types and sizes of appliances they connected to the system rather than by the volume of natural gas consumed. The yearly bill of a homeowner — including cook stove, lights, and a heating stove or two — might have been $40-50 per year. This seems modest enough, but one must remember that the glass manufacturers, who used hundreds of thousands of cubic feet of natural gas each day, paid but a few hundred dollars per year.

When Findlay's citizens realized the inequity in charges levied by the private suppliers, they urged the city to drill for natural gas and to create a municipal organization for the public good. An enabling Act was passed by the Ohio state legislature, and a special election held in Findlay during April, 1886, secured citizen approval for the issuing of bonds. The city was in the natural gas business, and, within a matter of a few months, several producing natural gas wells had been drilled and the streets of Findlay made ready for yet another set of gas mains.

The city began to compete with the private supplier, and the resultant rate war must have been the subject of great discussion in Findlay. Orton records that the competitors, in turn, halved one another's announced rates until a year's natural gas for a cooking stove could be had for $1.80. At this point the Findlay Gas Light Company brought suit against the Incorporated Village of Findlay in Hancock County Common Pleas Court (case number 4939). The company alleged that the Act passed by the State Legislature was defective, causing the municipality's authority to be improperly constituted. A second position of the company is more complex: the Findlay Gas Light Company argued that the tax monies paid by it to the city of Findlay were, in effect, used to finance its primary competitor when the city entered the natural gas business. The city, of course, was a tax-exempt body financed by public funds, thus compounding the competitive advantage over the privately-owned Findlay Gas Light Company.

The court ruled in favor of the city, but the company appealed the judgment to the Hancock County Circuit Court. The case was decided on March 4, 1887. In short, the court held that the city properly possessed "the corporate right and power to light the streets, alleys and public grounds . . . and furnish light and heat to the inhabitants . . ." (*Circuit Court Journal* No. 1, p. 70). The court also found that the Findlay Gas Light Company was, in fact, operating in violation of its corporate charter, which had been granted in 1871 for the purposes of manufacturing artificial gas from coal. Apparently, when the Findlay Gas Light Company bought out Oesterlin's group a few years earlier, they neglected to amend their corporate charter to include the development of natural gas resources. This might seem to be a very fine point of law, but, as will be seen later, it turned out to have great ramifications for Findlay's glass factories.

The Circuit Court's decision left the Findlay Gas Light Company without a basis to continue business and opened the way for the city to assume all natural gas operations. In a sort of paradox, the best natural gas wells in Hancock County were controlled by a private company which could not lawfully distribute the natural gas, and the city of Findlay, which had the legal authority over the natural gas, lacked the necessary producing wells and a full distribution system. The dilemma was resolved on October 10, 1887, when the city purchased the Findlay Gas Light Company for $75,000. From this point, natural gas in Findlay was under the complete control of the city. Governed by a Board of Gas Trustees, the city's operation moved quickly to issue more bonds and to expand its drilling operations.

The land syndicates continued to offer inducements to manufacturing interests, of course, but the resolution of the legal questions must have brought some stability to the situation. In the March 15, 1888, issue of *Pottery and Glassware Reporter*, a Pittsburgh-based publication, Findlay realtors McConica and Ely placed the following notice: See Figure A

The natural gas supply was quite probably more than adequate during the 1886-1888 period, but some problems began to emerge early in 1889. One of the Gas Trustees detailed the nature of the difficulty to a reporter from the Toledo *Commercial,* and the story eventually found its way into the September 26, 1889, issue of *Light, Heat and Power,* a trade journal which covered the technical and legal aspects of this emerging field. In the summer, natural gas pressure was strong and the supply plentiful, but cold weather, bringing about both an increase in demand for heating fuel and a decrease in pressure, was cause for concern. For reasons of safety, the gas pressure within the pipes to a home must be rather low, about two or three ounces, to prevent a rapid accumulation (and possible explosion) if a leak should occur or a low flame die out. Condensation of water vapor suspended in the natural gas is common within the pipes, and cold weather may cause freezing of the trapped water, often bringing about a blockage in the pipe, or, at least, a reduction in the natural gas flow. A further, more serious problem may develop when the natural gas well begins to bring oil and/or salt water into the distribution system during cold weather. The Gas Trustees were able to solve all of these problems by linking many producing wells in the piping system, so the winter of 1888-89 passed without any untoward incident.

During the summer of 1889, the Findlay Gas Trustees leased land in Biglick, Van Buren, and other townships. According to *Light, Heat and Power* (August 15, 1889) over 3,000 acres were involved, but "no one knows whether it is gas territory or not . . . There may be gas under these leases, and there may not." The editors went on to suggest that the Gas Trustees simply acquired the leases to prevent others from obtaining the rights to the land, a move easily regarded as a prudent business practice.

State Geologist Edward Orton had long been skeptical of the natural gas resources at Findlay. In his 1886 *Preliminary Report,* Orton observed that uncontrolled use and development could prove disastrous to Findlay: "The town and the immediate neighborhood give the best promise of containing a vast supply, but it must not be forgotten that it is a stored power. There is, in reality, a

---

Figure A

measurable amount of oil and gas available, and when this is gone, all is gone. No renewal will follow."

There were those who held different theoretical views on natural gas. They thought that the supply was infinite, arguing that natural gas is the product of a never-ending chemical reaction deep within the earth. In like manner, others persisted in drilling efforts, hoping against all evidence that natural gas was everywhere to found below the surface of the earth if one would only drill deep enough. Orton rejected these notions in his 1888 report with these words:

> The ardent wishes of the favored communities that have secured the new fuel, that their supply shall be perpetual, do not go far to prove that it will be perpetual. The so-called "theories" that are advanced in support of such a view, are utterly crude and baseless. Findlay gas will obey the law, *is obeying the law,* of all high-pressure gas that has ever been discovered. It is a stored product. The amount of it is measurable. Every foot withdrawn from the reservoir leaves the ultimate stock less.

He went on to note that Findlay was lighted, day and night, with more than 200 torches, each of which consumed well over a thousand cubic feet of natural gas per day. Early in 1890, Orton presented a paper at a meeting of the American Geological Society in New York City in which he predicted that northwestern Ohio's natural gas supply would be exhausted in less than nine years.

In March, 1890, *Light, Heat and Power,* quoting the Toledo *Commercial,* reported the demise of the Karg natural gas well:

> The great Karg, which at one time was capable of thrusting its fiery tongue half-way across the Blanchard River, lies there as cold and stiff in the jaws of death as any animal whose life had left it.

The article went on to relate that the failure of the Karg actually "caused the resurrection of a new life in the Board of Gas Trustees," for that group had been impelled to secure leases on even more possible natural gas lands to ensure a supply for the citizens of Findlay.

The acquisition of natural gas rights and the construction of a city-owned gas plant and distribution system in Findlay were not without expense, however, and some citizens were concerned about escalating costs. *Light, Heat and Power* reported in its October 24, 1889, issue that the bill for the city's gas plant had reached over $300,000 when only $30,000 had been projected for the facility. In Feburary, 1890, the same journal reported a contemplated advance in natural gas prices to Findlay's private consumers. A few months later, the matter of costs and rate changes was becoming critical; the problem was reported in the May 19, 1890, issue of *Light, Heat and Power:*

> . . . Findlay is growing tired of giving its gas away, and a recent advice from that city says:
>
> > The Board of Gas Trustees have appointed James G. Mills, William McKiness and E. B. Phillips as a committee to visit various cities using natural gas and ascertain the price these municipalities are charging manufacturers for gas, with a

view of readjusting the rates charged in Findlay, so that the burden of taxation may be more equally distributed. Under the present schedule, the private consumers pay 95 per cent of all the money taken in by the gas office, and the manufacturers the other 5 per cent, although the manufacturers consume 75 per cent of all the gas furnished by the plant. Notwithstanding this unfair condition, 2 of the Gas Trustees desire to increase the rates on the private consumers $45,000 for the coming year, and on the manufacturers only $9,000 in the aggregate. There will be a big protest from the people should this be attempted. If the Gas Trustees must have more money, the manufacturers, who have been having free gas for 3 years, are the ones to pay it. The people have been assisting these men to get rich long enough. These manufacturers, as a general proposition, are only sojourners, and in a few instances own property here. There is a great war just in sight on this question.

The "great war," if it may be termed such, began in late November, 1890. On November 28, 1890, the Board of Gas Trustees approved advances in the natural gas prices for many of the manufacturing plants in Findlay, including the glass tableware factories. The Columbia Glass Company had its yearly fee raised from $200 to $1300; the Bellaire Goblet Company's fee went from $400 to $3666.66 per year. Among the other manufacturers affected were the Electric Light Company, the Cleveland Target Company and the Findlay Clay Pot Company. The other glass factories involved were the Lippincott Glass Company (lamp chimneys), the Model Flint Glass Company, and the Dalzell, Gilmore and Leighton Company.

On November 26, 1890, the City of Findlay served each factory with a bill for December calculated at the new rates and announced that natural gas would be shut off on December 31 in those factories which did not pay their bills. The affected factories probably met as a group to plan their response. On December 30, 1890, each of the eight concerns petitioned Hancock County Common Pleas Court for temporary injunctions to restrain the city of Findlay from carrying out its notice regarding the shutoff of natural gas. The injunctions were granted, and the eight cases were assigned individual numbers (7294-7301, inclusive) by the Hancock County Common Pleas Court. Unfortunately, not all of the records of these proceedings have survived to the present day, but the materials and arguments in two of them — the Columbia Glass Company vs. the City of Findlay et al. (7294) and the case involving the Dalzell, Gilmore and Leighton Company (7295) — are most revealing to today's reader.

The suit filed by the Columbia Glass Company focused upon the contract that firm had signed on May 26, 1886 with Oesterlin's Findlay Gas Light Company. The attorneys for the glass factory argued that the contract was the sole reason for the glass company to build its plant in Findlay:

> . . . they located their plant at Findlay, made their said investments, employed laborers and skilled

workmen, and constructed, maintained and operated their said factory upon the faith and consideration of said contracts, and but for said consideration would not have made said location or investments. They further argued that the City of Findlay assumed this (and all other) natural gas contracts when it purchased the Findlay Gas Light Company in October, 1887.

Similar arguments appear in the briefs filed by the attorneys for the Dalzell, Gilmore and Leighton Company. The glass company first cited a contract with the Wyoming syndicate in which the factory received natural gas free of charge. When the Wyoming group sold some land and natural gas wells to the city on August 1, 1889, this contract was rewritten, calling for the Dalzell firm to pay $100 per year for natural gas for five years. The city had raised the price to $562.62 per month on November 28, 1890, just before the shutoff notice which precipitated the legal action.

In separate written briefs, the city of Findlay responded to the issues and allegations in each case. In the Columbia matter, the city noted its outstanding bond debt of over $360,000 and asserted that "it has become necessary to charge all consumers of natural gas and to require them to pay . . . a reasonable price." The city produced figures to show that over 90% of all natural gas consumed in Findlay was used by the factories, but that these customers paid less than 10% of the cost of the fuel. When the factories responded with, in effect, "a contract is a contract," the city retorted that the Findlay Gas Light Company lacked the corporate authority to sell natural gas, a point of law which had emerged in the lawsuit between the city and the Findlay Gas Light firm in 1887. Thus, the city concluded, it could not be expected to assume contracts which were illegally constituted. The promises of the various land syndicates, said the city, were merely "personal," and the city had no obligation whatsoever to honor them.

The legal manuevering made for exciting news, of course, and the Findlay *Morning Republican* carried lengthy articles detailing the various contracts in its January 8, 1891 issue. Before the cases were decided in late March, the Columbia Glass Company reached a settlement with the city, and its suit was withdrawn. On March 25, 1891, Judge Johnson agreed with the City of Findlay's position and dissolved the temporary injunctions held by the other seven factories. The city's power to set natural gas rates commensurate with costs was upheld, but the manufacturers were not yet ready to give up. Five of them, including the Bellaire, Dalzell, and Model concerns, petitioned the Hancock County Circuit Court to grant a new trial. The petition was taken under advisement on April 28, 1891, but the Circuit Court declined to order a new trial on June 23, 1891. The Dalzell, Gilmore and Leighton Company, probably acting for the other manufacturers in spirit, sought a temporary restraining order on the higher natural gas rates from the Supreme Court of the State of Ohio on November 24, 1891. The case was decided, in favor of the city once more, on February 25, 1892.

The city's legal victories would have been hollow indeed if the glass factories and other manufacturing interests had left Findlay without delay. Perhaps in response to this possibility, the city's Gas Trustees conferred with the various manufacturers soon after the Hancock County Circuit Court had rendered its decision. On August 28, 1891, the Findlay *Morning Republican* reported that the Gas Trustees and the glass manufacturers had met and worked out an agreement satisfactory to all. The new rate for natural gas was set at $10 per month for each "pot" being used in the respective company's furnaces. Even at full capacity, no factory would have incurred a bill greater than about $300 per month, far below the rates originally sought by the city when the fees were raised in November, 1890.

The natural gas supply problem eventually led both the Model Flint Glass Company and the Dalzell, Gilmore and Leighton Company to investigate the employment of oil as a fuel. The Model apparently decided to stay with natural gas, however, and the months of December, 1892 and January, 1893 proved most difficult for them. The natural gas pressure was low and some natural gas lines became obstructed. The city ordered the factories to bank their furnaces on December 24, 1892 and, by January 11, 1893, the natural gas situation was so severe that the Gas Trustees deemed it necessary to close the natural gas lines to the various glass factories. The Model Flint Glass Company sought an injunction or restraining order from the Hancock County Common Pleas Court, but Judge Johnson ruled against them. The firm had argued that a shutoff of natural gas would destroy their glassmaking pots, causing irreparable damage, so the judge allowed them to use sufficient natural gas "to prevent the pots from being chilled," to quote one Findlay newspaper. The crisis passed, and the Model Flint Glass Company installed an oil-burning system as a backup to natural gas. By March, 1893, a natural gas meter was put in the Model plant, so it continued to operate with at least some dependence upon the city's ability to supply natural gas.

The Dalzell, Gilmore and Leighton Company settled its account with the city by March 12, 1892, just a few days after the Ohio Supreme Court had declined to hear their case. The firm's progress in converting to an oil-burning system was widely reported in Findlay's newspapers during December, 1892-January, 1893, and this factory had its fuel system operational by January 12, 1893, when one newspaper reported that "a melt was made very successfully and the managers are more than pleased with their first day's work with oil." By March, 1894, the natural gas problems may have abated somewhat, for the Dalzell factory installed a gas-fired Siemans regenerative furnace. Some months later, on November 7, 1894, the factory requested a connection to the city's natural gas system for office heating fuel and lights only. In 1897, the firm signed a contract with the Standard Oil Company, and a few years later there were reports that the firm was using manufactured coal gas also.

Without doubt, the uncertainty over the natural gas supply as well as the legal battles concerning proper authority and equitable rates had some negative impact upon the glass tableware manufacturers in Findlay. There were, however, other factors which led to the waning of the industry. The 1880s and 1890s were a time of combination and pools in many manufacturing endeavors. When a number of previously independent firms merged, the obvious goals were reduction of competition and costs as well as control of output and, hence, prices.

Among the early pool rumors involving Findlay's glass tableware plants was this bit of speculation from the March 20, 1890, issue of *Crockery and Glass Journal*:

A dispatch from Findlay O. says that Edward Phelps, representing an English syndicate, has secured options on twelve of the fourteen glass factories at that place for $800,000. It is said that if the sale is effected, the capacity of the factories will be doubled.

The rumor was mentioned in *Pottery and Glassware Reporter* on the same date, but the editors commented rather dryly that the report was given "for what it seems to be worth, but [we] cannot vouch for its accuracy." Needless to say, no evidence whatsoever has emerged to substantiate this interesting story.

The forces behind a glass tableware manufacturers combination had emerged in Pittsburgh as early as 1884, when James B. Lyon led an effort to unite twenty-five members of the Western Flint and Lime Glass Protective Association, including several factories at Wheeling. In August, 1889, just after the July gathering of glass tableware interests at the Monongahela House Hotel in Pittsburgh, there were rumors about a proposed combination in *Crockery and Glass Journal*. These were mentioned from time to time both there and in *Pottery and Glassware Reporter*, but the first credible information appeared in February, 1891, when the United States Glass Company made application for a corporate charter in Pennsylvania.

Records in Hancock County show that the stockholders of the Bellaire Goblet Company met on December 15, 1890 to approve the sale of the plant to the United States Glass Company, although the sale was not completed until June 27, 1891. The Columbia Glass Company's stockholders met on June 25, 1891, and the factory was sold the next day. The consideration for both sales was one dollar.

The Bellaire and the Columbia really "joined" the United States Company rather than were sold to it. The company was, in fact, a merger of fifteen glass tableware factories. Each factory was designated by a capital letter:

Adams & Company, Pittsburgh, Pa.	Factory A
Bryce Brothers, Pittsburgh, Pa.	Factory B
Bellaire Goblet Co., Findlay, Ohio	Factory M
Central Glass Co., Wheeling, West Va.	Factory O
Columbia Glass Co., Findlay, Ohio	Factory J
Challinor, Taylor & Co., Tarentum, Pa.	Factory C
Doyle & Co., Pittsburgh, Pa.	Factory P
George Duncan & Sons, Pittsburgh, Pa.	Factory D
Gillinder & Sons, Greensburgh, Pa.	Factory G
Hobbs Glass Co., Wheeling, West Va.	Factory H
King Glass Co., Pittsburgh, Pa.	Factory K
Nickle Plate Glass Co., Fostoria, Ohio	Factory N
O'Hara Glass Co., Pittsburgh, Pa.	Factory L
Richards & Hartley, Tarentum, Pa.	Factory E
Ripley & Co., Pittsburgh, Pa.	Factory F

A. J. Beatty and Sons of Tiffin, Ohio (Factory R) joined the combine in January 1892, and the Novelty Glass Company of Fostoria (Factory T) was annexed in October of that year.

Several of the proprietors of both the Bellaire and the Columbia became officers in the new corporation. William A. Gorby and D. C. Jenkins, Jr., were both on the Board of Directors. Gorby was named purchasing agent of the United States Glass Company, and M. L. Blackburn was elevated to the mangership of the Bellaire plant, now known as Factory M. D. C. Jenkins, Jr., had the job of general superintendent over both the Columbia (Factory J) and Factory M as well as Factory T at Fostoria. Gorby moved to Pittsburgh in October, 1891, and Jenkins went to a new United States Glass Company plant, Factory U, at Gas City, Indiana, in February, 1893.

The natural gas shortage of December, 1892-January, 1893 had a great effect on both Factory J and Factory M. The plants banked their furnaces on December 10, 1892 and the Findlay *Morning Republican* reported that they would resume operations on January 15, 1893. When the shutoff notice came on January 11, 1893, the United States Glass Company retained Findlay attorney James A. Bope to serve notice on the Gas Trustees that they would be held personally liable for damages to the company's glassmaking pots. The trustees remained resolute, and the natural gas was cut off on January 12, 1893. Neither factory was restarted, despite rumors and newspaper speculation to the contrary. Within a few months, the fixtures had been removed from both plants and shipped to factories in the United States Glass Company.

The closure of the two Findlay-based United States Glass Company plants was probably a surprise to the residents of Findlay and Hancock County as well as an economic blow, for the two factories had large work forces. Nevertheless, the desire of the United States Glass Company to consolidate its interests was probably well-known among glass tableware manufacturers. This hope had been expressed in a new trade periodical — *China, Glass and Lamps* — as early as July 1, 1891, and it received further discussion in Feburary, 1892, when that same journal reported it as fact. In their study of the United States Glass Company, Heacock and Bickenheuser take up the matters of consolidation and relocation, and they note that the firm was greatly occupied by construction projects (at Glassport, Pa. and Gas City, Indiana) and labor union disputes in 1893-94.

Epilogue

The discovery of natural gas in Hancock County by Dr. Charles Oesterlin had a great impact on the development of industry in Findlay, especially the glass tableware business. A variety of inducements spurred activity and the plants were especially prosperous between 1886-1888, even while the city of Findlay fought to establish its role *vis a vis* natural gas in court. From 1889 on, there were problems with the flow and supply of natural gas. In 1891, a series of court decisions led to the establishment of a uniform rate per pot, but stability was short-lived, for the exceptionally cold winter of 1892-93 caused such a severe natural gas shortage that two large glass tableware factories, recent acquisitions of the United States Glass Company, closed for good. Another factory, the Model plant, was able to survive with an oil-fired back up system, but only the Dalzell, Gilmore and Leighton Company converted entirely to oil, continuing to add improvements in the early 1890s.

Chapter Two
GLASSMAKING AT FINDLAY

As the previous chapter has shown, the last quarter of the nineteenth century was marked by changes in the geographical location of American glassmaking interests, chiefly because of the utilization of natural gas for fuel. This efficient, easily controlled source of energy was, of course, a technological breakthrough which greatly improved glass melting furnaces as well as annealing procedures. Two other developments in glass technology had their impacts on Findlay's glass tableware plants—the replacement of lead glass with less costly lime glass, and improvements in the tools and techniques used in blowing or pressing glass.

The products of Findlay's five tableware factories were termed "pressed and blown glassware" by the industry. Most of the items were pressed glass, although lamp fonts were blown in all of the plants and the Dalzell firm's Onyx ware was blown. By the mid-1880s, the time of off-hand glass blowing was past. No longer were an individual's skills, augmented by simple tools, the determinants of glassware form. Cast iron moulds were used at Findlay to impart various shapes to the molten glass, and teams of workers (called "shops") divided glassmaking operations into a series of carefully planned steps. A few glass factories in the United States today produce pressed and blown glassware with essentially the same procedures as those utilized at Findlay. The most noteworthy of these is the Fenton Art Glass Company of Williamstown, West Virginia, which offers guided tours of its glassmaking plant.

The local newspaper or industry trade journal reporters who visited the Findlay factories almost always described the scenes there as "a hive of activity" or some similar metaphor. The casual visitor would probably have been frightened by the apparent chaos. The natural gas-fired furnaces roar incessantly. The pots and tanks glow red with molten glass and release heat without respite. Everywhere, workers bustle about, ranging from men with blowpipes giving shape to glowing gobs of molten glass to small boys scurrying to the lehrs with finished products upon their asbestos-covered paddles. There is a mystique, perhaps even some measure of romance, which surrounds the making of beautiful glass objects, especially those coveted by today's collector. In fact, the manufacture of pressed and blown glassware is a carefully-planned, well-organized set of procedures based upon economic and scientific principles.

In theory, a glass factory can be located anywhere. In actuality, glass plants are erected in places to take advantage of nearby raw materials, fuel or transportation facilities. Pittsburgh-area factories, of course, were near the timber- and coal-rich hills of Western Pennsylvania as well as railways and the steamboats on the Ohio River. The firms established in Wheeling and in Belmont County, Ohio, during the 1875-85 period had similar economic benefits, not to mention the ease of luring skilled glassworkers from manufacturing centers such as Philadelphia and Pittsburgh.

The factories in Pittsburgh, Wheeling and environs began to use natural gas for fuel in the early 1880s. A major source of supply was the natural gas and oil field around Washington, Pa. Several years passed before the pipelines were completed, and problems with the level of gas pressure were frequent, especially in cold weather. Since coal and timber were readily at hand, however, the factories were able to use alternate fuels without significant interruption in production.

Findlay's glass factories were literally on top of considerable natural gas supplies. Several of the firms had their own wells, and, as will be seen later, some purchased natural gas from the City of Findlay system. Railway transportation was at hand, as Findlay was crossed by major lines, including the Lake Erie and Western Railroad and the Toledo, Columbus and Southern Railroad. Delivery of raw materials such as sand and chemicals was convenient, and the railways made possible the fast shipment of products to all major points. Each glass plant was served by a siding or two from the nearby railroad.

A glass factory must be designed for efficient operation. Raw materials are unloaded from boxcars and stored near the mixing room. Sand for glassmaking should be both dry and free from foreign matter. Some chemicals used in making glass (such as soda ash) tend to absorb water vapor from the air, so they must be kept in containers with tightly-fitted lids. Unloading the sand and chemicals from the boxcars was hard work, indeed. Men used shovels to transfer the dry materials to large wheelbarrows or to carts pulled by horses or mules. Once inside the factory, these ingredients were dumped or shoveled into their respective containers.

Close to the storage area is the mixing room, usually termed the batch room by glassworkers. Here the components of glass are mixed in proper proportions by weight. The Findlay plants made soda lime glass, consisting of sand, soda ash, lime, and broken glass called cullet. Lead glass contains potash and lead oxide compounds, and this glass is a heavy, brilliantly clear colorless glass with a noticeable resonance. Lead glass is relatively soft and highly suited for cut glass production. Soda lime glass is somewhat less brilliant and less colorless than lead glass. The addition of decolorizing agents (usually manganese compounds) to soda lime glass batches helps to diminish these problems. Soda lime glass also hardens or sets up more quickly than lead glass, so the pressing or blowing operations must proceed with dispatch. Most important, soda lime glass is much more economical to make than lead glass. At 1890 prices, lead glass was three times as expensive as soda lime glass.

Adding small quantities of certain metallic oxides or salts to the batch will produce colored soda lime glass. Although the proportions of basic ingredients may be varied to some extent without changing the nature of the glass, even a small variance in the amount of a specific coloring agent may result in color changes which make the glass unsuitable for use. Iron and sulfur compounds create amber glass, and cobalt and copper compounds result in various shades of blue. During the 1880s and 1890s, individual glassmakers guarded their secrets and kept their favorite formulas to themselves. George W. Leighton, the glassmaker at the Dalzell, Gilmore and Leighton Company, took the rather unusual step of patenting the process by which Onyx glass was made. Patents on formulae or processes were the exception, however, and the procedures for making the usual transparent colors (amber, blue and green) were certainly common knowledge. Numerous factories made an opaque white glass (with aluminum and fluorine compounds) called opal (pronounced o-pal).

Batch ingredients were mixed by hand labor. Layers of sand were alternated with other chemicals poured into a wooden trough. The dry ingredients are then turned over with shovels and pushed about with hoes. The mixture is put into a wheeled batch cart to be taken to the pot or tank in which it is to be melted.

All of the Findlay glass tableware factories had pot furnaces fired by natural gas. These furnaces were circular in shape and are easily recognized by the tall smokestacks which resemble large inverted funnels. A pot furnace has its fire at the center of base, and the individual pots are arranged around the circumference. Pot furnaces may have as few as six pots or as many as sixteen set in individual arches. Findlay's largest tableware plant—the Dalzell, Gilmore and Leighton Company—had three furnaces with eleven pots each. The Columbia Gas Company, in contrast, was the smallest with its single thirteen-pot furnace.

Pots, composed of fire resistant clay, are made by hand in a lengthy process composed of building up and slow drying. The completed pot is beehive-shaped, and an access panel in the form of a half circle is provided near the top. Before placing in the main furnace, a pot must be heated slowly in a small auxiliary furnace to bring it to a temperature near that of the main furnace. When this has been accomplished, workers remove the pot from the auxiliary furnace, place it upon a cart, and manuever it into a vacant arch in the main furnace. "Pot-setting," as glassworkers call it, is a difficult job, but it must be done with some frequency, for the pots eventually crack or break from the intense heat and the chemical action of the materials used in glassmaking. About 1890, the Findlay Clay Pot Company was supplying the local glass plants with pots and other needed fixtures.

Once a pot is in the main furnace, cold batch is shoveled into it, and, after a day or two of heating, the ingredients have melted to form molten glass. The first melt in a new pot is not for regular production, because the pot's interior must be glazed with glass. This also serves to rid the pot of any foreign matter or other loose material which could contaminate subsequent batches. After the first melt has been cleaned out by a worker using a ladle, the pot can be used over and over again to make glass. A pot will last at least several months, but a particularly good pot might remain in place for nine months to a year. The furnace fire

plays against the backs and part of the bottom surfaces of the pots, and this heat must be kept constant.

Findlay's glass manufacturers feared any interruption in the supply of natural gas. If the main furnace loses fire, the molten glass may solidify in the pots, ruining both the glass batches and the pots. Damage may result to the interior of the main furnace, the flues, and even to the brickwork of the large smokestack.

In pot furnaces, the batch is heated indirectly by the natural gas flames. The furnace heat warms the walls of the pots and, in turn, the batch ingredients. A temperature of 2500 degrees is needed to melt the batch. In the 1890s, glass factories began to use tank furnaces in which the flame heats the batch directly. Some glass colors cannot be made in tanks because of the chemical effects of direct flame, but the tank furnace usually has a much larger capacity than an individual pot. The melting time is reduced in a tank furnace, and several tons of batch can be made molten in about twelve hours. Often, tanks are filled and the batch melted overnight, providing ample molten glass for the workers who arrive the next morning. These are called day tanks.

Groups of workers are organized into "shops." There are press shops and blow shops, and each consists of various skilled workers and unskilled workers called boys. Each shop is a well-coordinated team in which each member has specific tasks. Findlay's workers belonged to the American Flint Glass Workers Union, now one of America's oldest labor groups, which was founded in 1878. About the time the Columbia Glass Company began production, Local Union No. 74 of the AFGWU was chartered in Findlay; it remained until mid-1902, when the Dalzell firm ceased operations. Other local unions in Findlay served the lamp chimney employees.

The glass tableware manufacturers were "organized" also; they joined the American Association of Flint and Lime Glass Manufacturers, which had been formed in 1887 as an outgrowth of the Western Flint and Lime Glass Protective Association. The American Association was chiefly concerned with trade matters such as credit and terms of sale, so another group, the Associated Manufacturers, was begun about 1888-89 for the purpose of presenting a united front in negotiations with the AFGWU. The Associated Manufacturers was reorganized as the National Association of Manufacturers of Pressed and Blown Glassware in 1893; W.A.B. Dalzell served as secretary of this group for many years.

The labor union and the manufacturers' groups agreed on rules governing glassmaking procedures and conditions. Employees worked in shifts of about five hours duration called turns; in good times, a skilled worker might work eleven separate turns per week, the first beginning late Sunday evening and the last continuing through Saturday morning. Those engaged in packing glassware or maintenance had a somewhat more regular schedule, but the skilled glassworkers and their helpers might work from 6 to 11 a.m., returning to the factory for another turn from 6 to 11 p.m. In the interim, other shops labored from noon to 5 p.m., and some of these individuals worked the night turn also. The intense heat of glass factory work makes the afternoon turn the least desirable, especially during the hot summer months.

Each shop was required to produce a specified number of items during a turn. This number, called the move, is agreed upon by the local union and the plant management. The AFGWU published annual move lists for the major branches of the industry which provided the numbers for standard articles. In the pressed ware department, a shop making ordinary jelly tumblers (using two moulds) would make 800-1100 each turn. For larger pressed items such as bowls and compotes, the move might be 300-500, depending upon the shaping and/or fire-polishing required. Blown ware is a bit more difficult to make and usually involves numerous steps, so a move of 200-400 would be a typical range.

The pressed ware process begins when a skilled glassworker called a gatherer uses a solid metal rod (punty) to remove molten glass from the pot or tank. The punty, which is five to five and one-half feet long, may taper to a dull, rounded point or it may have a clay head about the size of a small doorknob. The larger the head of the punty, the more glass will be gathered when the worker inserts it into the molten glass and slowly rotates the punty. The molten glass must be free from air bubbles and from so-called stones, which are small bits of unmelted batch or extraneous material. The molten glass must also be homogenous in texture, without the somewhat more dense strings called cords which cause problems in working the glass.

The gatherer gauges the amount of glass needed for the pressing of a given article. If too little is gathered, the mould will not fill, and the imperfect item will have to be broken. This broken glass may be used as cullet in a subsequent batch, of course, but some needless waste has occurred.

The gatherer brings a gob of molten glass from the pot or tank to the side-lever press where another skilled worker, the presser, stands ready to see that the proper amount of glass enters the mould. When just the right amount has been allowed to flow from the end of the punty, the presser uses his scissor-like shears to sever the molten glass. The presser slides the heavy mould into proper position, and then he pulls the lever on the press. The strength of the presser is not a great factor, for the lever and springs of the side-lever press serve to insert the plunger into the mould. Nonetheless, the presser must have a feel for the work and be able to judge that the molten glass has filled the mould properly before he releases the side-lever to allow withdrawal of the plunger. If the plunger is inserted too long, the glass may cool too rapidly and adhere to the mould and/or the plunger. Special oils which resist high temperatures are used from time to time also. If the glass does adhere, production must be halted to clean the plunger and/or mould. If the plunger is withdrawn too soon, the glass will not have filled the mould, and the article will be incompletely formed.

Most of the time, however, the gatherer and presser have obtained the proper amount of glass, and the presser has allowed the plunger to withdraw at the right time.

Gatherer (in background) and presser.

The presser in action.

The presser (or an unskilled helper called a mould boy) slides the mould away from the plunger so the mould can be opened to remove the pressed glass article. When pressing soda lime glass, speed is of some importance, as this glass hardens or sets up rather quickly and must be worked more rapidly than lead glass. In essence, the introduction and widespread usage of soda lime glass in the last three decades of the nineteenth century necessitated an increase in the working speed of press shops and increased worker output compared to the days of lead glass.

Once removed from the mould, an article may undergo one or more finishing processes before being taken to the annealing ovens or lehrs. Tumblers and goblets are gripped around the base by a tool called a snap. The warming-in boy allows the intense heat of a small furnace known as a glory hole to fire polish the drinking edge. The article is removed from the flames of the glory hole and the snap is opened, permitting the carrying-in boy to lift the object with padded tongs, place it upon an asbestos-covered paddle, and take it to the lehrs.

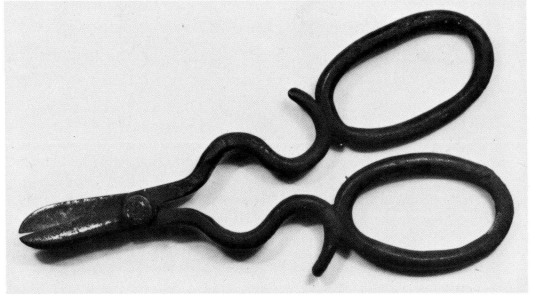

Presser's shears.

Finisher at work.

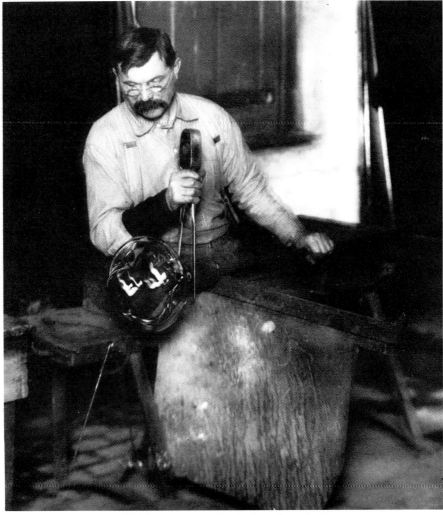

Finisher using pucellas to shape lamp font.

21

Water pitchers (called jugs) are warmed-in at a glory hole, and then a carrying-over boy conveys the reheated jug to the finisher, another skilled glassworker. The finisher sits on a bench with metal arms at his right and left. The long-handled snap which holds the jug rests across these arms, and the finisher is able to rotate the handle of the snap with one hand as he uses a tool in the other to shape a pouring lip on the jug. The finisher may reduce or enlarge the diameter of a pressed compote or bowl, and he is also responsible for crimping the edges of decorative items, either freehand with his versatile, spring-steel pucellas or with a foot-operated device which imparts a uniform pie crust edge to a bowl.

A particularly difficult finishing operation is the addition of handles to lamps or water pitchers. The gatherer must provide exactly the right amount of glass in a thick ribbon, and the finisher must attach it to the body of the article and use his tools to impart the right shape to the handle itself. When the finisher is satisfied, a carrying-in boy takes the item to the lehrs.

Any item made by pressing has its largest diameter at the area of the object where the plunger is inserted and withdrawn. In principle, the plunger is essentially cone-shaped to permit easy insertion and withdrawal. Usually, the plunger is perfectly smooth, and because items in various patterns are of standard sizes, the plunger may be used with a number of different moulds. Both the plunger and the mould become very hot during the pressing process as they absorb heat from the molten glass. The Findlay factories were equipped with a system of overhead ductwork (the so-called "wind" system) which allowed the presser to arrange flexible tubing and nozzles to direct forced air over the mould and/or plunger as needed to maintain a proper working temperature. The molten glass is very hot, about 2000 degrees, and the cast iron moulds work well when their surfaces reach 700-800 degrees.

The glassblowing process, like pressing, begins with the gatherer. He uses a hollow blowpipe to gather the right amount of glass, being sure that the molten glass is free of air bubbles or cords. Then, he hands the blowpipe to a skilled glassworker called a blocker, who is responsible for the initial shaping of the gob of molten glass. The blocker may stand upon an elevated platform as he rolls the molten glass on a marver, a flat steel plate with a smooth surface. He may use a semi-circular metal block in a tub of water for the same purpose, which is to assure that the gob of glass has been made symmetrical. When the blowpipe is held vertically, the molten glass should form a nearly perfect teardrop shape; this is called the parison.

The blocker will use his lung power to blow a puff of air into the parison to expand it slightly, or he may place the parison within a small spot mould and expand it there to impart a simple pattern to the molten glass. The spot mould is opened by a mould boy, and a warming-in boy removes and reheats the parison, depending upon the color effects the operation is designed to produce. A carrying-over boy conveys the heated, partially-shaped molten glass, still on the blowpipe, to the glassblower.

The blower brings the glass to its final or near-final shape. At Findlay, the glassblowers produced mould-blown

ware. Their lung power forced the molten glass against all inner surfaces of the iron mould. When the blower senses that this is complete, he simultaneously brings the blowpipe away from the mould and blows a final puff of air into the glass. This creates the blowover, a very thin bubble of extraneous glass which solidifies quickly and shatters immediately. The blowover is necessary to assure that the glass has filled the mould and to prevent the extra glass from dropping into the newly-formed article. The topmost edge of the article will be made smooth later, perhaps by reheating and/or finishing (just as in pressed ware) or by grinding after the glass has been annealed.

A mould-blowing process called paste mould involves both expanding the parison and rotating it within a mould. The pattern, if any, imparted by such a mould must be in very low relief. The blowpipe is removed by a procedure known as cracking off. The lamp fonts and other ware made via paste mould tends to be relatively free of the seams or mould marks found in blown ware, but paste mould ware is somewhat more difficult to make.

Onyx glass, Findlay's most famous product, is a cased (or layered) glass, made by a somewhat more complex glassblowing procedure. Leighton's patent claimed "certain new and useful Improvements in the Manufacture of Glassware," but the description of the process was intentionally general to prevent others from appropriating the techniques. After one color (usually opal) had been gathered and the block mould had been used to shape the glass, the gatherer inserted the parison into a pot or tank containing a different color of glass. The mould blowing process then took place, followed by warming-in to produce the characteristic metallic luster on the raised surfaces of Onyx glass. Problems are often encountered in annealing cased glass when the separate layers cool at slightly different rates.

Although most of Findlay's tableware products are pressed glass, both the blown and the pressed ware departments had their respective places in the five plants. Blown ware was both difficult and expensive to produce, but blown products have distinctive shapes or colors not possible in pressed glass. Economical mass production is easily obtained in pressed ware, and skilled finishers can impart shapes to pressed articles which make them nearly as interesting as blown ware. As described below, both pressed and blown ware can be treated in various ways after annealing has taken place.

When the carrying-in boy places a glass article in the lehrs, he completes the operations of the so-called hot metal shops, those groups of employees who work the molten glass. The carrying-in boy is responsible for keeping count of the numbers of items he places in the lehrs, thus ensuring that his shop has met the requirement of the move list.

The lehrs, or annealing ovens as they are sometimes called, gradually cool the glass articles to room temperature. The lehrs are about 900 degrees at the entry point. Findlay's lehrs contained shallow pans linked by metal chains. From time to time, the pans moved in succession to areas of the lehr in which lower temperatures were maintained by a series of baffles and heat regulating valves.

Within a few hours, the articles are cooled to room temperature. If the operation moves too quickly, the glass articles may crack because of internal strains. In extreme instances, the glass shatters spontaneously in the lehrs.

Natural gas was the perfect fuel for the lehrs. In earlier times, finished items were sealed up in heated enclosures and allowed to cool naturally, an imperfect process at best. Smoke from wood and coal fires may react chemically with hot glass, and washing or polishing may be necessary after the glass has cooled. Pipes and valves made natural gas flow easy to regulate, and the clean-burning fuel causes no problems with the glass. Even those Findlay factories which converted their pot or tank furnaces to oil preferred natural gas for the lehrs.

Findlay's glass tableware plants had their own mould-making shops. A cast iron mould can withstand temperatures of over 1000 degrees without developing cracks or flaws. The inner surfaces of the mould may be highly patterned and covered with intricate recesses, but they must be heat resistant and not cause the glass to stick to it. The mould may be composed of two, three or four hinged sections, and it must always open and close easily and fit together tightly.

After a designer or mouldmaker has prepared a sketch or working drawing showing a proposed glass article, skilled machinists begin to shape the cast iron pieces. Milling machines and lathes pare the excess metal, giving the iron a smooth finish, particularly on the inner surfaces. At Findlay, the power to run the machines was furnished by a large stationary engine connected to a series of shafts which probably rotated at ceiling level. Individual mould makers tapped into this power source by engaging floor-to-ceiling belts with levers at their work stations.

After the castings have been shaped and the mould sections fitted together for easy opening and closing, a skilled mouldmaker chips the desired pattern, in reverse, into the inner surfaces of the mould. He works slowly and carefully, using a small hammer and sharp chisels to create the pattern in the cast iron. Special care is taken so that the natural lines between mould sections will not be obtrusive when glass is pressed or blown in the mould. This is particularly important for pressed ware moulds, so the designer or mouldmaker may arrange elements of the pattern to minimize the visibility of mould marks. Warming-in may also diminish mould marks, as will fire polishing a goblet's drinking edge or a pitcher's lip.

Each of Findlay's glass tableware plants had its own mouldmaking shop. Even so, the need for new moulds was sometimes acute, and at least one independent operation, dubbed Arduser and Company, supplied moulds to the Model Flint Glass Company; a mouldmaker there, Henry Coons, made the mould for the Lord's Supper bread plate.

Pressed and blown glassware items are, of course, complete when they emerge from the lehrs. Many articles are simply packed and sold. Others may be subjected to one or more of three processes—engraving, etching and decorating—in order to produce some added effect.

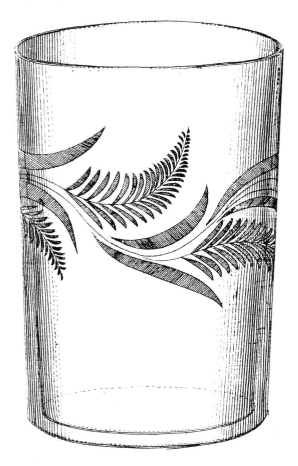 

Typical engraved tumblers (these were made at the Bellaire Goblet Co.).

Many American glass tableware factories offered engraved items during the last two decades of the nineteenth century, and the Findlay plants attempted to meet the competition, even though the designs were more or less standard in all of the concerns. Engraving is done with a thin copper wheel powered by the factory's stationary engine. The rapidly rotating wheel cuts into the surface of the glass, and the engraver moves the glass object quickly to achieve the desired design. Floral motifs were common, and most factories could supply their customers with elaborate scrollwork, initials or other representations. Sometimes complete pattern lines, such as Dalzell's 49D, were available either plain or engraved. Original advertising helps to document the various engraving styles of some of Findlay's factories.

Etching is a chemical process. Hydrofluoric acid reacts with glass, and the resulting satin finish is both pleasing to the eye and smooth to the touch. The glass object is exposed to the acid after wax has been applied to areas where etching is not wanted. After exposure, the articles are washed to stop the chemical reaction, and the protective wax is discarded. Of Findlay's glass tableware plants, only the Dalzell, Gilmore and Leighton Company seems to have used etching extensively.

Decorating consists of adding color to pressed or blown glassware after it has been formed and fully annealed. Workers (often women) paint the surface of the glass with the appropriate colored paint. Clear or transparent green articles were often decorated with gold, and the effect is quite pleasant. In order to bond the color to the glass permanently, articles were placed in a decorating lehr (about 1000 degrees) and gradually cooled to room temperature. If the decorating lehr is not employed, the paint deteriorates over time and may discolor or chip rather easily.

Once completed glass tableware items have been made, they must be carefully packed and shipped to waiting customers. It was the usual business practice to pack and inventory glassware soon after it was made, both to diminish breakage and to make possible timely shipments.

Glassware was shipped in wooden boxes or barrels of various sizes. Individual items were generally wrapped in thin paper (to keep them clean) and nested in straw to prevent contact during transport. Small items could be protected by pasteboard sleeves or partitions in a box. Thin-walled blown glassware needs more care in packing and protection than the heavier, thicker pressed wares.

Glass packers, such as the men and women in Findlay's plants, were paid a set wage per package; a quarter a barrel was the prevailing rate. The packers' jobs ranged from putting up boxes of 12-24 tumblers to packing "assortments" in large barrels called tierces. An assortment might consist of six pieces each of eight or more different patterns, so the packer would face the challenge of arranging several dozen variously-shaped articles within a single container.

Railroad sidings adjacent to the factories allowed the glassware packages to be loaded directly into the boxcars. Barrels were rolled up an inclined board, and boxes were carried by laborers. Full boxcars were integrated into trains, and they would reach their destinations within a few days. If the customer did not have a railway siding for unloading, a horse or mule cart was sent to the railway station so that the containers could be unloaded and transported to the customer's store or warehouse.

Findlay's glass tableware factories did not, as a rule, sell directly to retail customers. Showrooms at the plants were maintained for the convenience of visiting wholesale buyers, but these purchasers represented large-volume customers, and they bought glassware by the carload or in lots of dozens of barrels at a time. Each factory advertised in the trade journals—*Crockery and Glass Journal; Pottery and Glassware Reporter;* and *China, Glass and Lamps*—but their ads were often just patron notices to keep their name before the trade.

The most important glassware orders were generated by the firms' travelling salesmen, either on the road or at one of the regular trade exhibitions. Each factory had at least one salesman who journeyed from city to city, calling upon department store buyers or mail order wholesalers. The salesman probably carried glassware samples as well

DALZELL, GILMORE & LEIGHTON CO.

This photo was taken at the Monongahela House in 1899; note Amberette items at right.

as illustrated sheets showing his firm's products. In the 1880s and 1890s, the Pittsburgh-area factories would display their new glassware lines each January and July at a downtown hotel, usually the venerable Monongahela House. As tableware factories were established in Ohio and Indiana, they joined the exhibition. It was commonplace to find twenty-five or thirty firms at the hotel between 1886 and 1892.

The salesmen would take sleeping rooms with parlors, and the parlors would be furnished with tables and shelving covered with cloth. The buyers made their way from display to display, inspecting and admiring the new products and haggling over discounts. Each semi-annual exhibit lasted three to four weeks, and most factories had at least one new pattern line to introduce at each exhibition. The trade journals sent their reporters, of course, and much of the information in the next few chapters of this book is derived from their news stories.

Some factories sent glassware samples to manufacturer's representatives in the larger cities. These independent businesses maintained large showrooms and displayed the products of many different factories, adding to their displays as new samples came in. Buyers placed their orders with the representative, who, in turn, was paid a commission by the glass company. Glassware was shipped directly from the factory to the customer.

When a pattern line or other glassware product was a particularly good seller, it often turned up in the pages of catalogues issued by the wholesale mail order houses, such as Butler Brothers. This firm bought carload lots of pressed and blown glassware from many different companies, reselling it by the barrel to merchants in crossroads towns who could not afford to purchase large quantities. Butler Brothers catalogues are now valuable historical documents, for they help today's glass history researchers to determine both the intended uses and the relative prices of glassware. Nonetheless, the catalogues must be regarded with some care, as the Butler firm frequently created its own names for patterns which had enjoyed strong sales at an earlier time.

In every respect, Findlay's glass tableware factories were typical of their time. The advantages of good fuel and ready transportation allowed the plants to offer employment to many skilled glassworkers and others. The products of these factories were often similar to those of other pressed and blown glassware manufacturers, but a number of unique items will be discussed and illustrated in later chapters.

Chapter Three
THE COLUMBIA GLASS COMPANY

Findlay's first glass tableware factory was the Columbia Glass Company, located on Crystal Avenue near the Findlay Window Glass Company and adjacent to the railroad lines. The decision of some Pittsburgh-area glassmen to erect a tableware plant at Findlay was probably due to the efforts of the Findlay Gas Light Company. Its president, Dr. Charles Oesterlin, and its secretary, Elijah T. Dunn, entered into an agreement with David C. Jenkins, Jr., William T. Patterson, and Lucas Minehart on May 25, 1886 (this document was officially noted in the Hancock County Recorder's ledger on November 18, 1887). The agreement was simple enough; the glassmen would sell stock and construct the factory, and the Findlay Gas Light Company would drill natural gas wells to supply the factory's needs at a price of no more than $400 per year. If the gas wells were good producers, the factory's annual bill would drop to $200.

Pottery and Glassware Reporter broke the news of this new factory to the glass trade in its June 10, 1886 issue. Jenkins was identified as "night manager at McKee and Bros.' works," and Patterson was "head decorator at Thos. Evans & Co." These two, said the writer, "with five or six other practical workers, are organizing to build a tableware factory at Findlay, Ohio." A brief report appeared in *Crockery and Glass Journal* about a week later, noting only that "the proprietors are all of this city [Pittsburgh], and they intend to commence the preliminary operations shortly."

The "preliminary operations," of course, were the center of attention in Findlay during the summer and fall of 1886. On July 8, 1886, the Findlay *Morning Republican* contained this information:

> The flint glass works . . . will employ about eighty hands to start with. The factory will make flint table glassware of the first quality. It will be the largest factory in the state of its kind.
>
> The contracts . . . were recently let to Mr. Wm. H. Campfield, our energetic and genial court house contractor. The buildings alone are to cost $12,000. One will be 75 feet long by 75 feet wide and will have a patent pot furnace in the center at a cost of $5,000. A second will have two stories. The buildings will be completed before the 14th of October, and the shops will certainly begin work by the first of the following month.

News of progress on the factory's construction appeared regularly in the *Morning Republican* over the next several months, as did speculation about job opportunities at the glass plant. On August 16, for instance, the newspaper said that "the Columbia . . . will employ quite a number of women for decorating at from $10 to $15 per week."

The Findlay Gas Light Company drilled a natural gas well on the Columbia's land, as their agreement stipulated. The well, a strong one, was finished on September 13, 1886, and the Columbia's tall smokestack was completed just two days later. Another month was needed to install

the roof, and work on the factory's furnace occupied most of November. A reporter from the *Morning Republican* visited the new factory on November 17, 1886, describing it this way:

> There is a basement nine feet in the clear, extending throughout the building. The west part of this is to be used for storing sand and other material of a like character.
>
> Just east of this storing room is one 75 by 75 feet, to be used for a mixing room, in which the materials will be gotten ready for the pots. The north end of this room will also serve the purpose of an engine room.
>
> East of this is a large apartment, 40 by 125 feet, in which goods will be stored ready for sale. Connecting with this by a stair-way is another large room on the first floor, where the glassware is received from the lears and packed ready for shipment.
>
> Of the northeast corner of this apartment a neat office has been built, 16 by 22 feet, elegantly lined and sealed with elm and already handsomely furnished with office furniture. Connecting with this by means of a stairway is a small sample room on the second floor fitted up much the same as the office.
>
> To the west of the packing room are the lears, running through a room 50 feet long, and connecting with the furnace room at the other end. The lears are to be surmounted with four automatic fans. On their north-side are places for storing the moulds.
>
> South of the lear room, on the same floor, is an apartment for storing pots and another known as the batch room, the latter having an elevator connection with the basement and second floor.
>
> The most interesting portion of the building is the furnace room on the west side, 75 by 75 feet in dimensions. Here is the huge furnace with its 13 fire-clay pots. For the comfort of those who have to work here, cool air pipes are provided and there is also a large ventilator on the roof. In this room are also three small furnaces called "glory holes." In the northwest corner of this room are the doors to the pot and mould ovens, which form a small extension to the building.
>
> On the second floor is a large room for the storing of goods, another for the use of the decorators and a third for the mould-makers, the latter being supplied with 12 windows.
>
> There is a side-track from the L.E. & W. Ry., 700 feet in length, built for the special convenience of the Works.
>
> The building throughout is most substantially built of brick, the basement walls being of stone. Mr. W. H. Campfield, the energetic and competent contractor, completed it in the specified time and

in a manner entirely satisfactory to the company.

The gentlemen forming the Company have expanded about $40,000 cash in the building and its equipment and are entitled to the hearty gratitude and support of our people.

The factory will start with a large force of hands in about 20 days.

The new enterprise needed employees, of course, and more than 300 applications had been received by November 15, 1886. The jobs available to Findlay residents were unskilled or semi-skilled positions such as carrying-in and glasspacker, but a number of women were soon trained as decorators. The skilled workers who could blow or press glass were recruited from Pittsburgh and Ohio Valley factories by Jenkins and Patterson.

The Columbia Glass Company began production on December 13, 1886. The first items made, according to the *Morning Republican,* were "goblets, glass cans, lantern chimneys and sauce dishes." About a week later, the newspaper mentioned "colored and tinted ware" and said

that "visitors may purchase glassware in blue, old gold and other colors." Except for these brief notes, there is little information on the Columbia's products in local sources. This is not surprising, for the company depended upon large-volume wholesale transactions, and the patterns and items thus sold were advertised in the glass trade publications.

Even before the Columbia began production, *Pottery and Glassware Reporter* mentioned "novelties and fancy wares" as well as "tableware . . . and blown moulded goods" in describing the factory's output. On December 2, 1886, the journal said the Columbia would "make both blown and pressed table and bar ware in all the popular colors [and] lantern globes, specie and French jars, founts and lamps, and seed cups and bird baths."

A small ad appeared in *Pottery and Glassware Reporter* on December 2, 1886, but a full-page ad in the January 20, 1887 issue is more significant, for it mentions "new, original and elegant" patterns among the lines of pressed and blown ware, some of which were also engraved. In

Original letterhead from Columbia Glass stationery, August 18, 1891.

March, 1887, a modest patron ad began to run in *Crockery and Glass Journal.*

The April 4, 1887, issue of *Pottery and Glassware Reporter* revealed that the Columbia was "crowded with orders for both plain and engraved ware" and went on to list these products: Pattern No. 39 ("a grand success"); slipper; cup and saucer; No. 25 (Honeycomb-External) goblet; and P.D.N.Y. tumbler. The P.D.N.Y. tumbler cannot be identified for certain, but the slipper was probably the Puss-in-Slipper and the cup and saucer likely from the No. 54 line, Dew Drop, which is now called Hobnail Double-Eye.

Although the first items made in Hobnail Double-Eye were clear glass, all of the pieces listed on the next page also occur in both blue and amber.

1. bowl, 7″ d.
2. butter, covered
3. cake salver, 9″ d.
4. celery, 9″ tall
5. child's table set, four pieces
6. creamer
7. cup/saucer
8. dish, oblong, 7″ 8″
9. plate, 7″ d.
10. salt/pepper shaker
11. spooner
12. sugar, covered
13. toothpick
14. tumbler
15. water pitcher

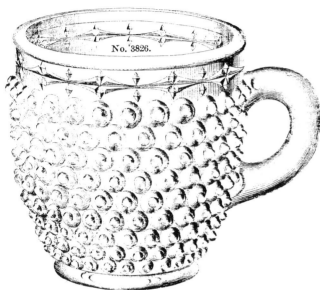

Old No. J., Dew Drop Cup.

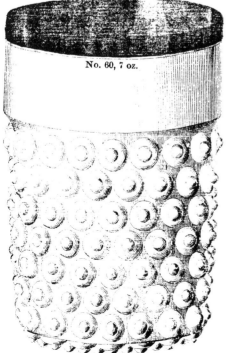

Old No. J., Dew Drop Capped.

Although the trade journals did not use the factory's pattern number for the new Dew Drop line, many of the various items made were mentioned. In addition to the cup and saucer, the tumbler was being made in October, 1887, and *Pottery and Glassware Reporter* for February 9, 1888, referred to the Dew Drop tableware pattern as "a full line," suggesting that water pitchers and other table items were available. *Crockery and Glass Journal* sang the praise of the Dew Drop line, calling it "one of the most striking examples of pressed ware that has yet been made. The name is a fitting one, as no dewdrop formed by nature could be more sparkling, clear and pellucid than this ware." A few months later, *Pottery and Glassware Reporter* called the Dew Drop toy set "the prettiest in the market" (May 10, 1888).

Pattern No. 39 is Little Bullet Band, termed Climax by some sources. An early catalog illustrated the four-piece table set in clear glass engraved with a graceful floral motif. The articles listed here occur only in clear glass, and any of them may be found with engraving.

1. bowls, 7″ 9″ d.
2. butter, covered
3. compotes, open/cov., 7″ 9″ d.
4. creamer
5. goblet

6. sauce
7. spooner
8. sugar, covered
9. tumbler
10. water pitcher, 2 sizes

8. salt/pepper shaker
9. sauce, 4″ d.
10. spooner
11. sugar, covered
12. syrup (tin top)
13. tumbler
14. water pitcher, 2 sizes

When the glass tableware manufacturers exhibited their new pattern lines at the Monongahela House in July, 1888, the specific products of the Columbia received scant coverage in the glass trade journals, although sales were reported to be "excellent." *Pottery and Glassware Reporter* mentioned Columbia's slipper ink [the Puss-in-Slipper] as well as a "vase lamp with brass cap or No. 2 collar" which was made in clear, amber, blue and black.

The exhibition held in January, 1889, was well-reported by the trade press, and the Columbia received these laudatory words from *Pottery and Glassware Reporter*:

The Columbia Glass Co. of Findlay, Ohio have their display in Room 74 with Mr. William J. Patterson in charge. This company was the pioneer in Findlay of flint glass manufacture which, as well as other branches of the business, has grown to such large dimensions. It is not saying anything too much to assert that they have kept up their end firmly and continue to maintain the prestige they established for themselves from the beginning.

A new pattern line, No. 59 Radiant, was introduced at this time, and the reporter noted a number of massive pieces in high quality clear glass, both plain and engraved. The following items are known to collectors today.

1. bowls, 6½″ 7½″ 8½″ d.
2. butter, covered
3. cake salver
4. celery
5. compotes, 5″ 6″ 7″ 8″ d. open/cov
6. creamer
7. goblet

Radiant goblet.

In July, 1889, yet another new pattern line, No. 14 Henrietta, was introduced by the Columbia. *Crockery and Glass Journal* called it "a masterpiece in pressed glass." This line became a mainstay of the plant's production, and ads showing a Henrietta bowl graced the pages of the trade journals for over two years, an extraordinary period, given the usual life of a new pattern in glass tableware circles. In July, 1890, *Pottery and Glassware Reporter* mentioned the Henrietta lamp, calling it "an elegant article . . . fit for a place on any table," and revealed that the Henrietta line had "a big sale and keeps its place among the foremost favorites." A number of pieces are known to collectors; all are in clear glass only, except for the 5″ vase, which has been found in green.

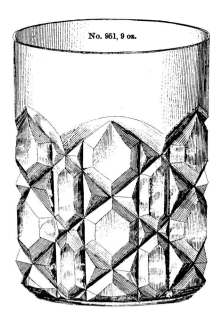

1. butter, covered
2. cake salver
3. celery holder, tall
4. celerys, flat, 5″ 8″ long
5. cracker jar

Henrietta pitcher and tumblers.

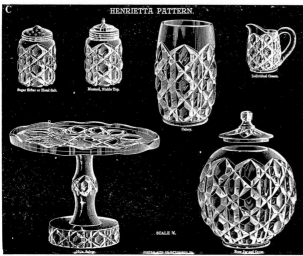

Glassware Reporter described it as "a square shield with bevelled edges, in imitation of cut ware, having strong dispersing power and [giving] a beautiful refractive effect" (January 8, 1891). A line of some seventy pieces was projected, but the next week's issue listed only the tankard pitcher, berry bowl and rose bowl. Just prior to the opening of the exhibit, a two-page ad appeared in the holiday issue of *Crockery and Glass Journal,* a sure indication that the Columbia had quite an investment in this pattern line. All of these articles have been found in clear glass:

1. butter, covered
2. compotes, 6″ 7″ 8″ open/cov
3. creamer
4. goblet
5. mustard jar
6. salt/pepper shaker
7. spooner
8. sugar, covered
9. sugar shaker
10. tumbler
11. water pitcher, 2 sizes
12. vase similar to pitcher

6. creamer
7. cup/saucer
8. lamp
9. miniature creamer
10. rose bowl
11. salt dip
12. salt/pepper shaker
13. sauce
14. spooner
15. sugar, covered
16. sugar shaker
17. syrup
18. tumbler
19. vases, 5″ 7″ 9″ tall
20. water pitcher, 2 sizes

The July, 1890, article quoted above also mentions other Columbia products: tankards (four sizes) in pattern No. 39, Little Bullet Band, and tankards (three sizes) in pattern No. 129, available both plain and engraved. No further descriptions were given.

Success often begets further success, and the January, 1891 exhibit at the Monongahela House provided the Columbia with the opportunity to introduce another pattern line. This was pattern No. 74, Banquet, now known as Thumbprint Block. A writer for *Pottery and*

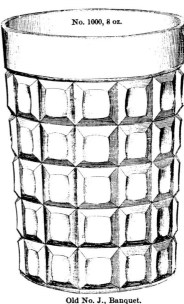

Old No. J., Banquet.

Thumbprint Block pitcher (a variant of Banquet).

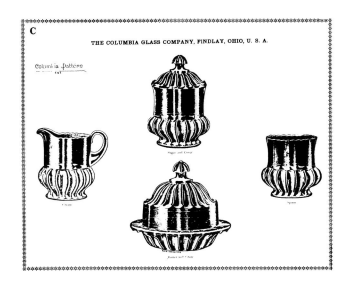

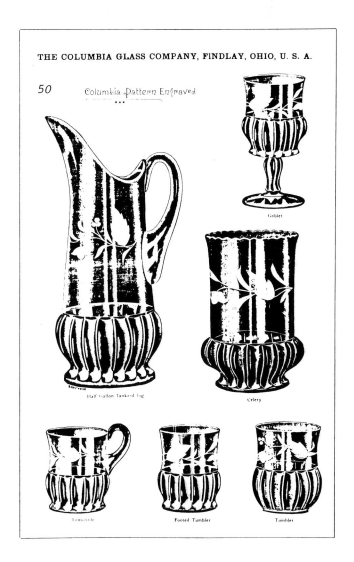

Early in 1891, the Columbia's D. C. Jenkins, Jr., became involved in an effort to consolidate a number of glass tableware factories. A reporter for the *Morning Republican* learned that Jenkins and other glassmen had applied for a corporate charter in Pennsylvania as the United States Glass Company (February 10, 1891). The Columbia's stockholders voted to put their factory into the combine in June, 1891. This consolidation did not have any immediate impact upon the firm's marketing practices, however, and William Patterson displayed the Columbia's wares at the Monongahela House in July, 1891.

Crockery and Glass Journal described the pattern line being introduced merely as "crystal tableware" (July 23, 1891). The new trade paper — *China, Glass and Lamps* — reported the line's name to be "Columbia" and revealed that the pattern was available in about 40 pieces, both plain and engraved. The pattern number, if any, for this new line is not known. An early catalog called it simply "Columbia pattern" and illustrated the four-piece table set in clear glass. These pieces are known in clear glass:

1. butter, covered
2. celery, 8″ tall
3. creamer
4. spooner
5. sugar, covered
6. tumbler

THE COLUMBIA GLASS COMPANY, FINDLAY, OHIO, U. S. A.

Sugar Duster.   Mustard.   Wine   Tooth Pick

Columbia Pattern
***

Mug   10 In. Salver.

No. 851, 8¼ oz.

Old No. J., Columbia.

Columbia celery (engraved).

The next sales season began in January, 1892. By this time, the United States Glass Company was fully organized and its plants were in operation. Jenkins was a member of the Board of Directors, and he was supervisor of both Factory J (the Columbia) and Factory M (the Bellaire Goblet Company) in Findlay, as well as Factory T in nearby Fostoria. The United States Glass Company decided to eliminate the mouldmaking shops in the individual fac-

tories and to centralize this important function in Pittsburgh. The Columbia's chief mould hand was John R. Bridges, who had come to Findlay with his wife and three sons in August, 1886, to oversee this aspect of the firm's construction; he resigned in December, 1891. According to the *Morning Republican,* Bridges was going to open a machine shop in Findlay in hopes of perfecting a knitting machine he had invented. He rejoined the U.S. Glass Co. as superintendent of the two Findlay plants in August, 1893, and in May, 1894, the company appointed him general manager of a new factory at Gas City, Indiana.

The United States Glass Company had twelve new pattern lines on view in January, 1892, and they advertised them one at a time in the various trade publications during the first four months of 1892. The U.S. Glass Company apparently numbered its initial pattern lines consecutively, beginning with the five-digit number 15,001. The first pattern credited to Factory J, the former Columbia Glass Co., was 15,006, now known as Pointed Jewel. Full-page ads appeared in two issues of *China, Glass and Lamps* (April 13 and 20, 1892). A number of articles, all in clear glass, are found in this pattern.

1. bowl, 8″ d.
2. butter, covered
3. cologne bottle with stopper
4. creamer
5. cup/saucer
6. goblet
7. honey dish
8. jelly compote, 4″ d.
9. sauce
10. spooner
11. sugar, covered
12. tumbler
13. water pitcher, 2 sizes

Pointed Jewel assortment in U.S. Glass Co. catalog, ca. 1892-3.

Pointed Jewel assortment in U.S. Glass Co. catalog, ca. 1892-3.

Pointed Jewel was also made at Factory N, formerly the Nickel Plate Glass Company of Fostoria, but it has not been possible to determine which particular items were made in each plant.

Two other patterns in the 15,000 series are also attributed to Factory J—15,014 (Heavy Gothic) and 15,021 (Broken Column). Heavy Gothic was also made at the King Glass Company (Factory K) in Pittsburgh, and Broken Column must also be credited to the Richards and Hartley firm (Factory E) of Tarentum, Pa. Thus, it is not possible to ascertain exactly which items were made at Findlay.

These articles have been found in Heavy Gothic; all are known in clear glass, and the lamp has been seen in green. The clear glass pieces may be engraved.

1. butter, covered
2. cake salver, 9″ d.
3. celery
4. compote
5. creamer
6. goblet
7. lamp
8. sauce, 5½″ d.
9. sauce, 4″ d.
10. water pitcher, 2 sizes
11. wine

Heavy Gothic spooner.

Heavy Gothic assortment in U.S. Glass Co. catalog, ca. 1892-3.

Broken Column was a rather extensive line; many of the clear glass items listed below have been seen with attractive ruby-red decor.

1. bowl, 6″ d.
2. butter, covered
3. cake salver, 9″ d.
4. creamer
5. compote
6. cracker jar
7. celery
8. celery tray, 7″ long
9. goblet
10. plates, 5″ 7″ 8″ d.
11. salt/pepper shaker
12. sugar shaker
13. tumbler
14. water pitcher
15. wine

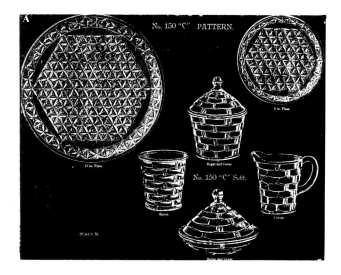

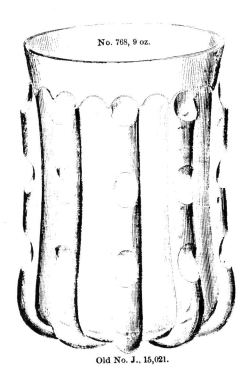

No. 768, 9 oz.

Old No. J., 15,021.

Broken Column tumbler.

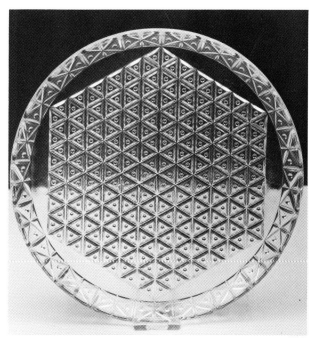

Plate for Bamboo Beauty line.

In their study of the United States Glass Company, Heacock and Bickenheuser illustrated several other patterns made at the Columbia plant. Pattern 150C was dubbed Bamboo Beauty by them, and an unnumbered line called simply "Shell" (or Shell on Ribs) was also shown. They also showed a catalog sheet showing the Tycoon line, a pattern identified earlier by Don Smith.

Bamboo Beauty was apparently a short line. Beside the four-piece table set (covered butter, creamer, covered sugar and spooner), the only items known today are round plates (6″ and 10″ d.). Similarly, Shell on Ribs has just five items known today, the four-piece table set and a pickle castor. The Tycoon line was somewhat more extensive. In addition to the four-piece table set, the following items occur: celery, 9″ tall; cracker jar; two sizes of cups; tumbler; and water pitcher.

Bamboo Beauty covered sugar bowl.

SHELL SETT.

Shell Sugar and Cover.

Shell Spoon.

Shell Cream.

Shell Butter and Cover.

Mug.

Cup.

Sugar and Cover.

Spoon.

Cream.

Butter and Cover.

Don Smith's fragments also make possible the attribution of Double Beetle Band, Columbia's File and Mitred Frieze (originally called Eldorado) to the pattern lines made at Columbia. Mitred Frieze and Columbia's File are found only in clear glass. Just a few articles are known in Mitred

No. 1012, 9 oz.

Old No. J., Eldorado.

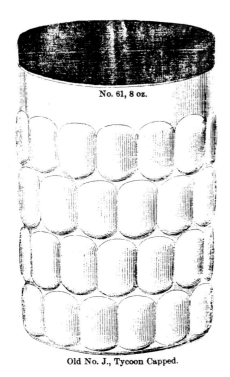

No. 61, 8 oz.

Old No. J., Tycoon Capped.

Mitred Frieze celery.

Frieze—celery; covered butter; goblet; spooner; and tumbler. Columbia's File was a longer line; these items occur:
1. butter, covered
2. compote
3. creamer
4. plate, 10½" d.
5. spooner
6. sugar, covered
7. syrup
8. water pitcher

1. butter, covered
2. creamer
3. cup
4. mug, child's
5. spooner
6. sugar, covered
7. tumbler
8. water pitcher
9. wine

File spooner.

Double Beetle Band pitcher.

Double Beetle Band seems to have been a major line. All of the items listed in the next column occur in blue and amber as well as clear glass.

Smith's fragments enable the authentication of several other patterns, all of which occur in clear glass only. An attractive four-piece child's set is known in Long Jewel,

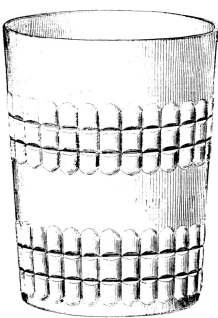

Double Beetle Band tumbler.

No. 991, 7½ oz.

Old No. J., 27.
Bevelled Block and Fan tumbler.

and tumblers have been seen in Bevelled Block and Fan and Funnel Rosette. Three items have been found in a pattern called Prince Albert—goblet, tumbler and water pitcher. Two other patterns, Rip-Rap and Prism, are known only in fragments, but collectors continue to search for whole items.

Funnel Rosette pitcher and Prince Albert pitcher.

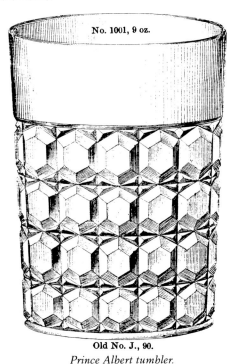

No. 1001, 9 oz.

Old No. J., 90.
Prince Albert tumbler.

In addition to producing extensive pattern glass sets, the Columbia Glass Company also made some "novelties," as they were known in the glass trade. The Puss-in-Slipper has already been mentioned, but readers should be aware that it may be found in clear, amber and blue glass. The Dog Vase is an interesting item, as are the round Pet Dishes (6″ d.) which may depict either a cat or a dog. The Boy/Girl Cups fit comfortably on the Acorn Saucer, and they probably were sold as sets.

Pet Dishes (6″ d.).

Dog Vase

Like many glass factories of the 1880s and 1890s, the Columbia turned out quite a number of rather plain mugs, jelly tumblers and bar goods, most of which are impossible to list and are attributable to the firm through careful study of fragments. One such product was Honeycomb-External, in which a goblet and tumbler are known. Fragments indicate two other similar motifs, Honeycomb and Honeycomb Shield.

After the Columbia was absorbed into the United States Glass Company, the trade press carried numerous reports of rumors and other speculative comments on the combine's future. There were the usual problems of coordinating a large organization, of course, and labor difficulties with the American Flint Glass Workers Union were frequent (and sometimes lengthy) at some individual factories. Nonetheless, the first annual report of the U.S.

Boy/Girl cups with Acorn saucer.

Capped mugs and jelly tumblers; Tycoon mugs at left.

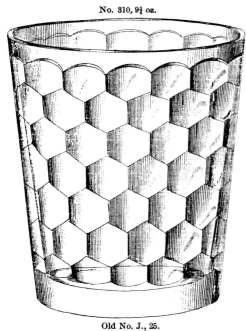

No. 310, 9¾ oz.

Old No. J., 25.

Honeycomb-External tumbler.

Glass Co., issued by president Daniel C. Ripley, was optimistic. Dividends were paid to holders of preferred stock in March, 1892, and sales reports at the end of June, 1892, amounted to about $2.5 million for a six month period.

When Factory J resumed operations after the summer stop on August 15, 1892, the plant was running 16 shops, its "full capacity," according to the *Morning Republican.* In September, the newspaper reported that glassware was being shipped to Hamburg, Germany.

In early December, 1892, however, all Factory J employees were notified of "an indefinite shutdown," in the words of *Crockery and Glass Journal.* The *Morning Republican* told its readers that the cessation of work was "for the purpose of invoicing and taking stock," but, in fact, December 10, 1892, was to be the last day of glass production in the Columbia plant.

Superintendent D. C. Jenkins Jr. continued to be optimistic in early January, 1893, but the situation soon became clear: natural gas pressure, already low, was dropping in the cold weather; political pressure was being exerted on the city's Gas Trustees to put the needs of Findlay's citizens above those of the manufacturers. On

January 10, 1893, the trustees decided to cut off the gas to the United States Glass Company's plants. D. C. Jenkins Jr. tried to delay the shutoff, informing the trustees that the plant hoped to convert to fuel oil and threatening legal action if the factory's pots and furnaces were damaged. On January 11, the U.S. Glass Company's attorney, Col. James A. Bope, told the trustees that legal steps would be taken against them, but the trustees reaffirmed their decision.

On the morning of January 12, 1893, the natural gas supply was turned off. Attempts to obtain a court injunction were not successful. The *Morning Republican* took note of the large monetary loss to the glass interests of the town and stated that "the shutting off of the gas from the factories made so little difference in pressure that the mercury gauge in the gas office showed absolutely no change throughout the day."

Within a few weeks, D. C. Jenkins Jr. and John Bridges had left Findlay for other responsibilities with the U.S. Glass Co. Despite some newspaper reports later in 1893 and on into 1894 that "the old Columbia glass factory" would begin anew, nothing of the kind was to happen. The pioneer glass tableware factory in Findlay, the Columbia Glass Company, was no more.

Chapter Four
THE BELLAIRE GOBLET COMPANY

The Bellaire Goblet Company was a well-established, successful Ohio Valley enterprise which moved to Findlay during the natural gas boom. The company began in 1876, and, during the late 1870s and early 1880s, was a prominent glass manufacturer in the Bellaire-Bridgeport-Martins Ferry area, just across the Ohio River from Wheeling. An ad in an April, 1881, issue of *Pottery and Glassware Reporter* listed the factory's capacity at "15,000 dozen pieces per week." As the company name implies, this firm made primarily pressed glass goblets and other stemware.

The coming of the Bellaire Goblet Company to Findlay was well-reported in the local press. On March 14, 1888, the *Morning Republican* revealed that M. L. Blackburn, W. A. Gorby and John Robinson were in town, "investigating the advantages of Findlay." About two weeks later, the newspaper carried a full account of the decision to move to Findlay:

The glass industry of the United States is rapidly centering at Findlay. The unrivalled inducements of free sites and free fuel are causing old established manufactures to leave their present surroundings and come to Findlay.

Three gentlemen representing the Bellaire Goblet Company of Bellaire, Ohio, visited this city and were shown about by our public-spirited citizens. They had been at Fostoria and intended going from there to Indiana to seek a new location for their works.

When they came to Findlay, they expected to remain only a few hours. But they were so attracted by the thrift and enterprise of the people, by the undoubted success of the numerous factories now in operation, etc.

This morning [March 27, 1888] Messrs. Blackburn and Gorby arrived, and today are fixing up a contract to be signed for the removal of the Bellaire Goblet Company's factories to Findlay.

The Bellaire Goblet Company is one of the oldest established and most extensive glass factories in this country, and manufactures all kinds of pressed table ware.

The factory will be built with 30 pots, being two and a half times as large as the Columbia Works. About 300 hands will be employed, making it the most extensive glass factory in northwestern Ohio.

Work on the buildings will be commenced at once, so that the factory will be ready to commence operations next August.

In every respect, this is one of the most important factories yet secured to Findlay, and we may well congratulate ourselves on the fact that our city was chosen as the best point in all the natural gas territory.

A few months earlier, *Pottery and Glassware Reporter* reviewed the glass trade and wrote that the Bellaire Goblet Company had had "by far the best year in the history of the factory." Without doubt, the firm's decision to relocate in Findlay was undertaken with the hope of making a good business even better. The proprietors of the Bellaire did not decide to move in haste, however, for *Crockery and Glass Journal* had reported a year earlier that the Bellaire men were considering "several towns in the interior of Ohio" (March 3, 1887). There were some problems with natural gas in the Ohio Valley during the first few months of 1888, notably weak pressure and rising costs, so it was not unexpected when the decision to relocate was announced to the trade in *Crockery and Glass Journal* (April 5, 1888). The Dalzell, Gilmore and Leighton Company decided to move about the same time, so these two Ohio Valley manufacturers may have acted with one another's knowledge if not in concert.

Construction of the Bellaire plant began in late April, 1888. By mid-May, the walls were completed, and the June

Letterhead from old location; note that "Findlay" is printed over the previous address.

44

BELLAIRE GOBLET WORKS.

11, 1888, issue of the *Morning Republican* announced that the roof was ready for its slate coverings. The factory, located on College Street east of Fox, was large, housing two fifteen-pot furnaces and a sizeable mouldmaking shop.

Many fixtures were transported from Bellaire to Findlay. *Pottery and Glassware Reporter* noted that twenty-five railway cars were needed to bring side-lever presses and other equipment to the plant. Glassworkers came to Findlay for jobs; many were from the Bellaire area. On August 7, workers filled three coaches on the Baltimore and Ohio. This influx put a strain on Findlay's available housing. The Bellaire Goblet Company built a boarding house near the plant for some seventy-five workers. The house was run by the Kilgore family, who had maintained a similar facility in Bellaire.

Glassmaking commenced about August 13, 1888, and, a month later, the *Morning Republican* reported carload shipments going to New York and other Eastern cities. The factory had a work force of about 300, ranging from skilled glassworkers to engravers and decorators as well as the young boys who performed a variety of tasks.

A shortage of boys concerned the glass manufacturers in Findlay, and the Bellaire Goblet Company advertised for "boys over 12 years old" as early as November 1, 1888. In January, 1889, W. A. Gorby led a contingent of glass manufacturers to Columbus, where the group urged the State Legislature to reject a change in the child labor law which would have set a minimum age of 14. The manufacturers needed inexpensive child labor to remain competitive with glass factories in other states. The *Morning Republican* discussed the situation and observed that "many boys are learning a good trade, who would otherwise be loitering about the streets."

Documenting the glass patterns and items made by the Bellaire Goblet Company at Findlay in no easy undertaking, for many moulds had been shipped from Bellaire. Some patterns and articles were, no doubt, made in both plants. The Bellaire did not exhibit at Pittsburgh in July,

New letterhead, ca. late 1888.

45

1888, and no special advertising appeared in the trade papers. In fact, the Bellaire's ads were limited throughout the fall of 1888, mentioning only "stem and bar ware."

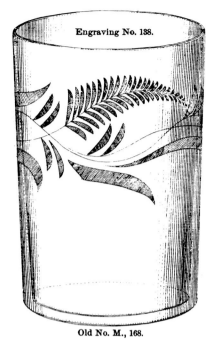

Engraving No. 138.

Old No. M., 168.

Engraving No. 139.

Old No. M., 167.

Engraved tumblers, typical designs made at the Bellaire Goblet Company.

In January, 1889, the company participated in the semi-annual trade show at the Monongahela House hotel. A writer from *Pottery and Glassware Reporter* visited sales-man Andrew W. Boggs in Room 178 and penned this description:

> The staples and specialties made by this company are pretty widely known to the trade, and include everything known in the business in stem and bar ware. They have added some novelties this season besides. The general assortment is very large, and there are a number of new ideas in shapes and engravings that the trade will find worthy of note.

Among these may be mentioned a handsome line of ale tumblers, imitation cut, castor, spice tray and a milk punch that holds about a quart, and is in great demand. They have enlarged their line of bar sugars by the addition of 7, 8 and 9 inch to the 6-inch, which was formerly the only size made. They are of polka dot pattern and very clear and attractive. This is a very extensive assortment and it surpasses all ordinary reason that there could be anything in the line of bar goods or drinking glasses of any sort that it does not contain, and that of every imaginable size, design or conformation.

Unfortunately, the account quoted above is very circum-spect, but some tentative conclusions can be made. First, the factory's products seem to have been rather plain goods in clear glass, since no colored ware is mentioned. Second, the absence of any pattern names or numbers means that extensive pattern lines had not yet been developed. Little material is available to document the Bellaire's production in early 1889, for the trade journals carried only a patron ad. On April 15, 1889, the *Morning Republican* noted that 15 engravers were employed at the Bellaire, so some engraved ware was obviously being made. The newspaper said the firm was "running steadily" on May 7, 1889. Two days later, catastrophe struck.

The headline of the May 9, 1889, *Morning Republican* tells the story: "BELLAIRE GOBLET WORKS FIRE." An extensive article detailed the event and assessed its impact upon Findlay:

> The most destructive fire in the history of Findlay occurred at an early hour this morning, sweeping out in a few moments the accumulations of a busy lifetime.
>
> The mammoth Bellaire Goblet Works, one of the largest glass factories in the United States, is a mass of ruins, and nearly 300 working people are thrown out of employment.
>
> About 2:30 this morning, A. F. McGarrell, the night watchman, discovered a fire breaking out . . . near the center of the main buildings.
>
> Upon seeing the blaze the watchman did his best to extinguish it with the appliances at hand, but the flames gathered headway in spite of all his efforts. He then endeavored to call up the fire department by telephone, but failed.
>
> Some of the attaches [sic] living near were aroused, but in a few minutes that this required, the fire had gained immense headway, and the entire inside of the building was ablaze, and the flames were travelling with unheard of fury.
>
> The ware rooms were broken open and an effort made to get out some of the stock, but by the time 50 barrels had been rolled out, the heat had grown so intense, that all hopes of saving anything had to be abandoned.
>
> In the meantime someone uptown had seen the blaze and gave the alarm at the Central engine house. The chemical and the No. 1 Steamer re-sponded promptly and put the horses on the gallop all the way, but arrived too late to do any good.

There was plenty of water from Howard Run, but the fire had already done its work. The roof and all the interior work, as well as the ware rooms, were completely destroyed, and only the brick walls and furnaces were left standing. The engine house was partially destroyed, while the mixing room and the boarding house and stables, all frame structures, were not damaged at all.

The company had an unusually large stock of goods on hand, as the sales have been comparatively dull this season, and a stock was being accumulated for the summer shut down, which will begin July 1st.

In the ware rooms there was stacked up 10,000 barrels of packed ware, valued at between $35,000 and $40,000. In the factory there was a stock estimated at $5,000 to $10,000; this was all destroyed, so that the loss on stock amounts to between $40,000 and $45,000.

The loss on the buildings and machinery will amount to about $60,000, making the total loss in the neighborhood of $100,000. The insurance amounts to about $60,000, and the net loss will reach $40,000. All the policies are all in the safe, which cannot be opened until to-morrow; the exact amount cannot be determined.

One of the worst features of the fire is the fact that such a large number of persons are thrown out of employment. The employees number 285, and the weekly payroll amounted to between $2,000 and $3,000.

The majority of these people have nothing saved up to fall back upon, and it is so late in the season that they cannot well get work elsewhere. Many families are depending upon them, while others are here with board to pay, and no way of making anything to pay it with.

The factory has been working night and day until two weeks ago, when the night work was suspended. Had there been a force working at night,

the disastrous fire would never have occurred, as the men are thoroughly drilled to fight fire, and there were plenty of appliances to put it out with. But as it was, there was only one man about the buildings, and his efforts were not sufficient to subdue the flames.

An interview was had with the President, M. L. Blackburn, and the Secretary, W. A. Gorby, who appeared to feel greater concern for the people thrown out of employment, than they did for their own great loss.

They would not say particularly whether the works would be rebuilt or not saying they could not determine upon anything until they saw how their insurance was coming out.

They are placed in an unfortunate position, as they have no stock to commence next season with, and all the moulds will have to be remade. This alone is a great undertaking. They will have the walls left standing intact, and the furnaces are apparently in good condition.

The company, which run in Bellaire for a number of years, removed here and erected their buildings only last summer, and started to work on the 13th of August, 1888. They had not yet completed their first year's run.

The Findlay *Weekly Jeffersonian,* in a May 16 story, revealed that more than 1.5 million goblets had been destroyed. Also of note is this newpaper's mention that two other Findlay glass factories—the Hirsch-Ely Window Glass Company and the Findlay Window Glass Works— had burned within the past eighteen months.

Fire was a constant fear of glass manufacturers, of course, since the highly flammable natural gas was both a benefit and a danger. Piping systems were far from perfect, and leaks sometimes caused an accumulation of explosive natural gas. Factory buildings contained much wood, and the constant heat from the pot furnaces, glory holes and lehrs made the wood very dry indeed. Finished glassware was packed in wooden containers, and the packing room

had its own fire hazards, straw and paper. When these conditions were combined with the usually inadequate state of fire-fighting equipment, it may be fortunate that even more glass factories did not suffer a similar fate.

About ten days after the fire, the *Morning Republican* made this declaration: "We are pleased to be able to announce that arrangements have been made so that the Bellaire Goblet Works . . . will be rebuilt on a larger scale than before." The insurance adjusters completed their evaluations in late May, and, by June 10, the Bellaire had begun to rebuild. The *Morning Republican* observed that "every man who can use a shovel, a saw and a hatchet have pitched into it in earnest." On August 19, 1889, the massive reconstruction job was finished, and the factory began producing glassware once more.

Even as the plant was being rebuilt, the Bellaire Goblet Company continued to receive orders. The firm was present at the Monongahela House exhibit in July, 1889, although no account of its display appeared in the glass trade journals. The patron ad continued to run in the weekly *Pottery and Glassware Reporter,* and by October, 1889, the ad said simply "Have Resumed Operations. Your Orders Respectfully Solicited."

By January, 1890, the Bellaire Goblet Company was obviously back to normal. *Crockery and Glass Journal* (January 2, 1890) mentioned "two new lines for this season and they are . . . good ones."

Two weeks later, the Bellaire and several other glass manufacturers announced a joint display of their goods at 1220 Main Street in Wheeling. An illustrated ad of the latest Bellaire pattern, now called Giant Bulls Eye, appeared at this time, so it must have been one of the two new lines. These clear glass items are known in Giant Bulls Eye:

1. butter, covered
2. cake salver
3. cracker jar
4. creamer
5. goblet
6. lamp
7. pickle dish
8. pitcher
9. spooner
10. sugar, covered
11. tumbler
12. vases, 7″ 8″ 9″ tall

No. 21 Castor Set.

Giant Bulls Eye pitcher.

Giant Bulls Eye cruet with stopper.

Giant Bulls Eye tumbler.

*Queen's Necklace Vase and condiment set
(oil bottle with salt and pepper shakers).*

Queen's Necklace bowl.

The new pattern line for 1891 was probably Queen's
Necklace, and a cologne bottle in this pattern appeared in
an ad in *China, Glass and Lamps* (December 17, 1890).
Giant Bulls Eye remained in production also, and the four-
piece table set, called simply No. 91, was illustrated in
China, Glass and Lamps during the late spring (May 6,
1891).

Queen's Necklace cruet with stopper.

Queen's Necklace was an extensive line, and these clear glass articles occur:

1. bowl, 10″ d.
2. butter, covered
3. cake salver
4. castor set (2 oil bottles and toothpick)
5. celery
6. cologne bottle
7. compote, open, 10″ d.
8. creamer
9. cruet
10. goblet
11. lamp
12. oil bottles
13. pitcher
14. rose bowl
15. salt/pepper shaker
16. spooner
17. sugar covered
18. syrup
19. tumbler
20. vases, 8″ 9″ 10″
21. wine

When the July, 1891, exhibit opened at the Monongahela House, the Bellaire Goblet Company was represented by Albert R. Leazure, whom *Crockery and Glass Journal* called "young, but a promising salesman." The new pattern line was No. 151, and *China, Glass and Lamps* said it was "the most varied they have ever displayed" (July 8, 1891), which would seem to indicate a sizeable line, probably Stars and Bars.

Our "GORGEOUS" Half-Dollar Assortment.
Three Diamond Sparkling 50-Cent Bouncers.

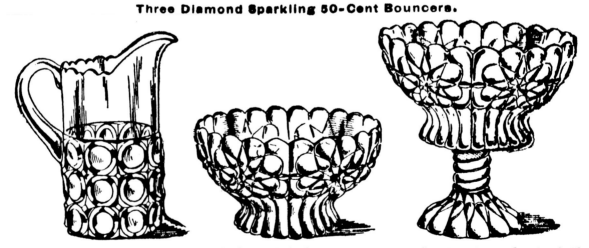

An assortment containing not only three of the largest pieces ever offered to the trade at a half dollar selling price, but of a pattern attractive beyond description and in shapes useful at every daily meal. One package of these goods as a sample purchase—ordered, if you please, on our recommendation—will surely lead up to the consumption of many lots by your customers in the future.

THE " GORGEOUS" ASSORTMENT INCLUDES:

⅓ doz. 10-inch, very deep bowls, footed, standing 10 inches high.
⅓ " 10 " heavy and deep round dishes.
⅓ " 3-quart water pitchers, massive and beautiful.

..... Order here. *(A total of 1 doz. in pkg. Sold only by pkg.)* **Price, $3.40 Doz.**

Giant Bulls Eye pitcher and two pieces in Queen's Necklace.

50

Stars and Bars was made in clear glass as well as amber and blue:

1. butter, covered
2. cake salver
3. creamer
4. cruet
5. goblet
6. lamp
7. mug, miniature
8. plate
9. railroad car (2 sizes)
10. salt/pepper shaker
11. sauce
12. sherbet cup
13. spooner
14. sugar, covered
15. tray

During the summer of 1891, the United States Glass Company was being organized. The Bellaire's stockholders had met at Findlay on December 15, 1891, to authorize the sale of the firm to the combine, but the transaction did not take place until June 27, 1891. W. A. Gorby was a member of the U. S. Glass Company's board of directors, and on July 23, 1891, the *Morning Republican* announced that he had been appointed purchasing agent for the combine. M. L. Blackburn succeeded Gorby as factory manager. Later in the summer, the Bellaire's bookkeeper, L. G. Batelle, assumed the same duties for the U.S. Glass Co. and moved to Pittsburgh.

In September, 1891, the mould shop at the Bellaire (now called Factory M) was closed down, although the factory continued to make glass "day and night," to use the *Morning Republican's* phrase (September 15, 1891). Boys were in short supply, and the newspaper often ran this sort of notice: "Forty boys, 14 years or older, needed immediately, Bellaire Goblet Works."

Production continued at Factory M throughout 1891 and most of 1892, but it is difficult to ascertain exactly what was being made. Like the Columbia (Factory J), the Bellaire's output was being sold through the general offices of the United States Glass Company. Heacock and Bickenheuser do not attribute any of the 15,000-series patterns to Factory M. Only a few other patterns are linked to Factory M — Beaded Blocks; Bellaire; Log and Star; Queen's Necklace; and Stars and Bars — and most of these were probably in production before the Bellaire became part of the United States Glass Company.

Stars and Bars cake salver.

Stars and Bars cruet.

Log and Star cruet with stopper.

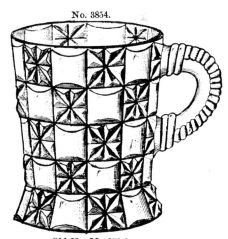

No. 3854.

Old No. M., 373-0.

Log and Star mug.

Log and Star was made in amber and blue as well as clear glass:
1. cordial
2. cruet
3. goblet
4. mug
5. pitcher
6. salt/pepper shaker
7. sherbet cup
8. tray

Log and Star pitcher.

The Bellaire Goblet Company made quite a variety of stemmed goblets, cordials and wines, of course, and many of them can be authenticated from Smith's fragment research. These patterns occur in clear glass and other colors as indicated: Acme (amber and blue); Barrelled Block; Beaded Rosette (amber); Coachman's Cape; Cottage; Doderly Thumbprint; Diagonal Block Band;

(Text continued on Page 71 pictures on Page 69)

Acme goblet.

Beaded Rosette goblet.

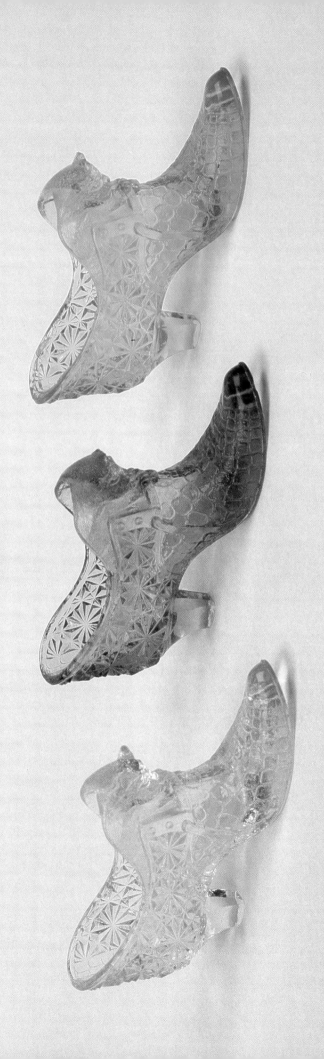

Puss-in-Slipper novelties in clear, amber and blue (Columbia Glass Company).

53

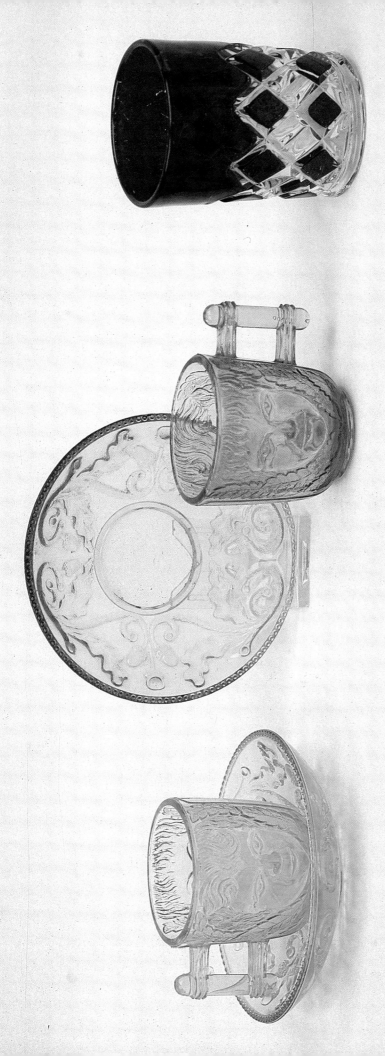

Boy/Girl cups with Acorn saucers in blue and amber (Columbia Glass Company): Block and Double Bar ruby-stained tumbler (Findlay Flint Glass Company).

Assortment of Floradine ware: note the whitish foliage and the all-over satin finish, the latter obtained by acid etching (Dalzell. Gilmore and Leighton Company).

Three extraordinary Onyx pieces, in "various color effects," as mentioned in original advertising (Dalzell, Gilmore and Leighton Company).

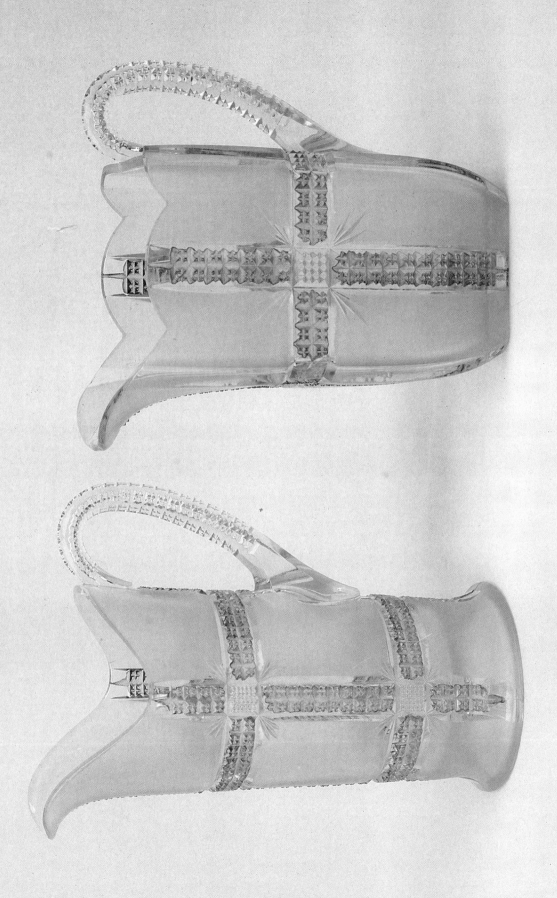

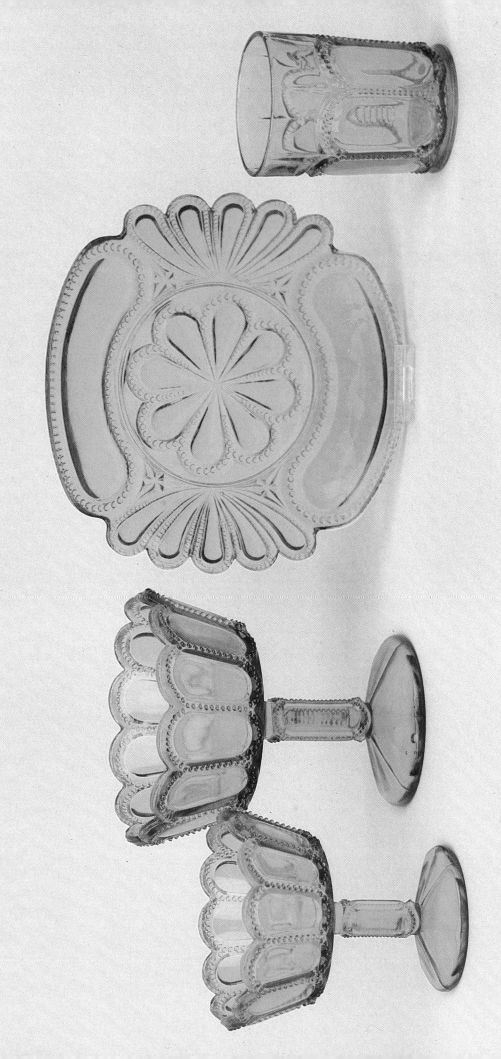

Emerald green Beaded Medallion open compotes, large plate and tumbler (Dalzell, Gilmore and Leighton Company).

Blue Currier and Ives round plate, Balky Mule motif (Bellaire Goblet Company).

Stars and Bars condiment set—cruet, shakers and tray—in amber (Bellaire Goblet Company).

Clear and blue Pig paperweights (Bellaire Goblet Company).

Three Shoes matchholders in clear and blue (Bellaire Goblet Company).

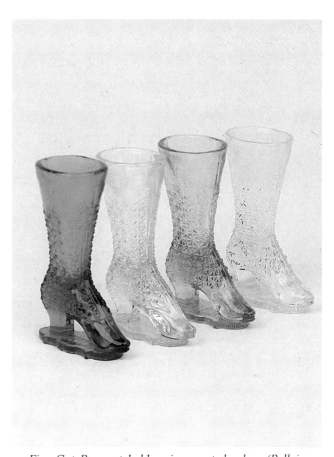

Fine Cut Bouquet holders in assorted colors (Bellaire Goblet Company).

Clear Chick toothpick holder and blue salt shaker (Bellaire Goblet Company).

Amberette square sauce dish and boat-shaped relish (Dalzell, Gilmore and Leighton Company).

Hobnail Double-Eye punch cups in blue and amber (Columbia Glass Company).

Panelled Jewels goblets in amber and blue (Bellaire Goblet Company).

Panelled Nightshade goblet in amber and Currier and Ives goblet in blue (Bellaire Goblet Company).

Russell Flower Pot
(Model Flint Glass Company)

Blue Edna covered sugar bowl (Dalzell, Gilmore and Leighton Company).

Double Beetle Band child's mugs in blue and amber (Dalzell, Gilmore and Leighton Company).

Shell on Ribs pickle castor in clear (Columbia Glass Company).

Stippled Forget-Me-Not wines in clear and amber (Findlay Flint Glass Company).

Coachman's Cape goblet.

Diagonal Block Band goblet

Gargoyle goblet.

Girl with Fan goblet.

Knurled Band goblet.

Janssen goblet.

Jelly tumbler with tin lid; Moerleins goblets.

Doderly Thumbprint goblet

Notched Rib goblet.

Panelled Jewels goblet.

Panelled Long Jewels goblet.

Panelled Nightshade goblet.

Panelled Potted Flower goblet.

Pittman goblet.

Thumbprint and Twist Stem goblet.

Tapered Prisms goblet.

Fern Spring goblet

Cottage goblet

Triangles and Flute Fans goblet

Continued from page 52

Fern Sprig; Gargoyle; Girl with Fan; Graduated Diamonds; Knurled Band; Janssen; Moerleins; Notched Rib; Panelled Jewels (amber and blue); Panelled Long Jewels (amber and blue); Panelled Thousand Eye; Pittman; Thumbprint and Twist Stem; Tapered Prisms; and Triangles and Flute Fans. Clear glass goblets and celery holders are known in both Panelled Nightshade and Panelled Potted Flower. Fragments of a few other goblet lines have been found — Horizontal Rib; Internal Lens; Rib Swirl; and Rings. Fragments of a cruet in the Pillow with Point Bands pattern have also been unearthed.

An interesting pattern, Currier and Ives, is verified by fragments as are Thumbprint Triangles and Button and Button. Only the clear glass cruet occurs in Thumbprint Triangles, and the Button and Button line consists of just four clear glass articles: bowl, creamer, sauce and pitcher. Currier and Ives was made in amber and blue as well as in clear glass, but these hues were also produced when the plant was in the Ohio Valley, so it is not possible to

determine which of these articles are exclusively Findlay-made:

1. celery
2. compote, open
3. cup/saucer
4. goblet
5. mug
6. pitcher, 2 sizes
7. relish, boat-shaped, 6″ long
8. tumbler
9. trays, 9½″ 12¼″ d. (Balky Mule motif)
10. wine
11. wine carafe

Currier and Ives tray, Balky Mule motif.

Several other patterns can be traced to Findlay. Milton includes the goblet, sherbet cup and wine as well as a castor stand with toothpick holder. Bellaire's Round

Thumbprint Triangles cruet.

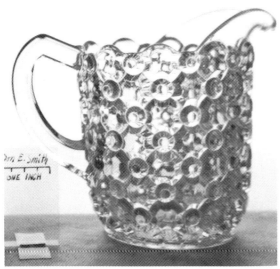

Button and Button creamer.

Milton goblet.

Bellaire Basketweave cruet.

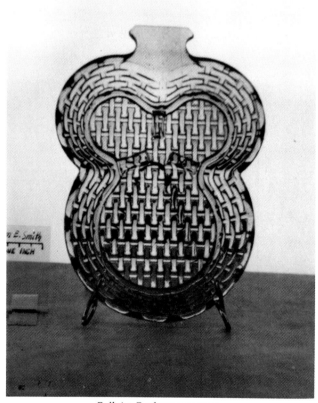

Bellaire Basketweave tray.

Bellaire Pittsburgh perfume bottle with stopper.

Hobnail cup is known in both clear and amber. Bellaire Basketweave occurs in amber, blue and clear, and these items are known: creamer, cruet, goblet, oil bottle, salt/ pepper shaker, toothpick holder and tray. The Bellaire Pittsburgh pattern includes these items in clear glass: cruet; several sizes of compotes; perfume bottles with stopper; pitcher; and tumbler. An unusual lamp base in the Bellaire Pittsburgh pattern is also known in blue and

Our "HOME CIRCLE" 50-Cent Lamp.

With Patent Safety Brass Socket.

Made up in the same strong manner as the "Evening" lamp, but of a larger size (standing 12 inches high to the collar) and made to take a No. 2 burner

Packed 4 of each color—opal, blue and amber.

Making a total of 1 doz. to bbl. (Sold only by bbl.)

... Order here.

Price, $3.50 Doz.

Bellaire Pittsburgh lamp base.

amber. Another pattern, Bellaire Bullseye, is somewhat more extensive:

1. butter, covered
2. cake salver
3. compote
4. creamer
5. cruet
6. cup/saucer
7. goblet
8. rose bowl
9. spooner
10. sugar, covered
11. toothpick
12. vase
13. wine set (carafe, round tray)
14. wine

Although stemware and a limited number of tableware sets seem to constitute the bulk of the Bellaire's output, some attractive novelties were also made. None of these was mentioned in any of the trade periodicals, but all have been verified from fragments dug at the factory site.

Several novelties depict items of personal clothing: the Corset toothpick and the Three Shoes matchholder. Both occur in clear, amber and blue, and the Three Shoes is also known in black glass. The Baby Shoe comes in clear only. The high, button shoe Fine Cut Bouquet Holder occurs in four hues—clear, amber, blue and vaseline—and sharp-eyed collectors note that there are "right" and "left" shoes, either of which may be found with or without the distinctive "B & H" advertising!

Three Shoes matchholder.

Corset toothpick.

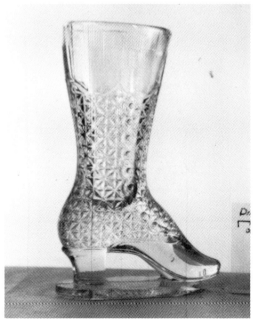

Fine Cut Bouquet Holder.

73

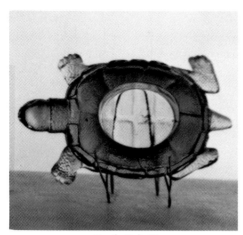

Turtle Salt Dip.

Pig on Railroad Car.

Other novelties use the form of animals: Turtle salt dip and Pig paperweight. Also known is the unusual Pig on Railroad Car, 5½″ long. The well-detailed Clock Face matchsafe is very rare.

Factory M's demise occurred at the same time as that of Factory J (the old Columbia) on December 8, 1892. The furnaces were banked in order to save fuel and keep the pots warm. Although the *Morning Republican* said that both Factory J and Factory M would re-open on January 15, 1893, U.S. Glass Co. officials came from Pittsburgh to Findlay on January 4 for a meeting with Findlay's Gas Trustees. The trustees' position was steadfast: the factories had received adequate notice to convert to fuel oil, and the natural gas was to be turned off on January 12, 1893. The glass company's attorney, Col. James A. Bope, was in contact with the Gas Trustees until the last moment, but, by January 13, the fires were out.

In late January, 1893, there were reports that the natural gas supply was improving, and the *Morning Republican* predicted that the U.S. Glass Company's plants "will in all probability be running within the next few weeks." A month later, however, the situation was different. Machinery had been removed from the Bellaire's buildings; the boiler and stationary engine, along with the entire mixing house, were shipped to Gas City, Indiana, where a new U.S. Glass Company plant was under construction. Plant manager John Robinson, who had been a charter stockholder in the Bellaire's Findlay operation, left for Zanesville, Ohio, where he founded the Robinson Glass Company.

The history of the Bellaire Goblet Company, especially in its later stages, is similar to that of the Columbia Glass Company. Both began as independent operations, and the Bellaire specialized in pressed glass stemware and goblets. Both were successful individual concerns in the late 1880s, but they cast their futures with the newly-formed United States Glass Company. The conglomerate saw its fortunes elsewhere, however, and the problems with natural gas in Findlay probably hastened the corporation's decision to discontinue the plants there.

Chapter Five
THE DALZELL, GILMORE AND
LEIGHTON COMPANY

The history of the Dalzell, Gilmore and Leighton Company is the story of a highly-successful glass manufacturing concern. The company was Findlay's longest-lived glass tableware factory, spanning the years from 1888 to late 1901. Like the Bellaire Goblet Company, the Dalzell enterprise was a well-established Ohio Valley glass company which relocated in Findlay during the natural gas boom. Three Dalzell brothers—Andrew, James and William—and Pittsburgh banker E. D. Gilmore were the owners/operators of a glass factory in Wellsburg, West Virginia, which was called Dalzell Brothers and Gilmore. They had had a plant at Brilliant, Ohio (across the Ohio River from Wellsburg), earlier in the 1880s.

James Dalzell

W. A. B. Dalzell

The negotiations to bring this factory to Findlay can be traced to a brief social note in the *Morning Republican* (January 7, 1888): "James Dalzell and E. D. Gilmore were guests of D. C. Jenkins yesterday." A few months later, this item appeared: "W. A. B. Dalzell of Wellsburg, W. Va. is in the city." Two days later, on April 9, 1888, the *Morning Republican* carried this headline: "Dalzell Brothers & Gilmore Glass Factory Will Remove From Wellsburg W. Va. To The Brilliant City." A long article gave the details:

> Saturday evening about six o'clock the contracts were signed and sealed between syndicates of this city and Messrs. Dalzell Brothers and Gilmore, by which the latter contract to remove their immense factory from its present location at Wellsburg, West Virginia, to Findlay.
>
> The company agrees to put up buildings here to cost $27,000 and furnaces, pots and machinery to the value of $33,000 more, making a total investment in the plant of $60,000. To carry on the business they will have a working capital of $100,000.
>
> The new factory will be located on the Wyoming Place addition, on the line of the Nickle Plate railroad, five blocks north of the Bellaire Goblet Company.
>
> There will be two 15 pot furnaces giving employment to not less than 300 hands, that being the minimum number permitted by the contract.
>
> Work on the buildings will be commenced as soon as plans are drawn, and pushed forward rapidly, so that the factory may commence work by the 1st of August, next.
>
> Dalzell Brothers and Gilmore stand at the head of the pressed tableware trade of this country. It is an old, established house, with abundant capital, and has always made itself felt in the glassware market.
>
> Not only will it do Findlay good by the direct results of the $150,000 paid out in labor in the course of a year, but the influence of the name will be far-reaching, and prove a great advertisement.
>
> The factory makes a specialty of fine engraved tableware, producing some beautiful designs, and leading the trade in this branch. From 15 to 30 high-salaried engravers are employed in designing and decorating.
>
> The credit for locating this great industry belongs to a great extent to those live and energetic new citizens of Findlay, Messrs. A. L. Baron and Mr. Rufer, of the Ohio Lantern Company, who have ever proved themselves untiring for the Brilliant City.
>
> They have been ably assisted by those newer acquisitions to our list of manufacturers, M. L. Blackburn and W. A. Gorby, of the Bellaire Goblet

Company, who by their knowledge of the trade and high standing in business circles were enabled to exert a large influence.

These gentlemen are now thoroughly identified with Findlay's interests, and are working earnestly and intelligently for the good of their adopted city. E. T. Dunn, John Scott, T. H. McConica, W. B. Ely, D. T. Davis, W. W. Cunningham, and others, also worked unceasingly to secure this valuable acquisition to our manufacturing interests.

Without doubt, M. L. Blackburn and W. A. Gorby were instrumental in bringing the Dalzell plant to Findlay. Their Bellaire Goblet Company had negotiated its own future only a few days earlier, signing its contracts March 29, 1888.

Although the *Morning Republican* (April 17, 1888) reported that the Dalzells would close up the Wellsburg factory "at once . . . so as to give their entire attention to the building of the works here," the Wellsburg operation continued for some months. The original plans for the structure at Findlay were also changed; instead of two 15-pot furnaces, the factory would have three 11-pot furnaces. On June 4, 1888, the management team was altered when William Leighton, Jr., and his son, George W. Leighton, joined the firm. The company name was the Dalzell, Gilmore and Leighton Company, and the enterprise was incorporated in West Virginia.

The factory buildings were nearly finished by August, 1888, when the Wellsburg plant was shut down and many of its fixtures were moved to Findlay. On September 6, the *Morning Republican* reported that one 11-pot furnace was in operation. Between September 4-10, about 150 glass workers emigrated from Wellsburg to Findlay. A second furnace started in late September, but the third was not fired until December, 1888.

Throughout much of the factory's life, there were difficulties with the unskilled workers or "boys," as they were called. On October 8, 1888, some boys went on a short-lived wildcat strike, summarized below by the *Morning Republican*:

The strike consisted of about 20 boys, engaged in "picking up" and "mould shutting," and they demanded an increase in pay. They were getting 50 cents a turn and demanded 60 cents.

•The company refused to advance the wages, as the boys asked for more than is being paid anywhere in the country.

The strike was engineered by a half dozen "bums" from Wheeling, who persuaded and intimidated the other boys into joining them.

At midnight there was some fear of trouble, as the strikers gathered about the doors of the factory and kept those who wanted to work from entering, but today, all is quiet.

The men about the works all denounce the action of the boys as unreasonable and unwarranted, and they are especially down on the boys for causing them to lose a day's work.

The factory's major problem, however, was having sufficient numbers of boys. In late November, 1888, about 30 orphan boys came to Findlay from the St. John's Home in Brooklyn. The Dalzell firm rented a large house and

Factory, ca. 1889.

hired a matron to look after the boys. The need for their labor was constant, and the *Morning Republican* often carried notices similar to this: "Ten girls wanted to work as decorators and 15 boys needed immediately. Report to manager, Dalzell glass company."

Because the company had moved its operation, the early Findlay products were identical to lines made previously at Wellsburg. A small ad in *Pottery and Glassware Reporter* (November 3, 1887) during the Wellsburg days mentioned patterns 9D, 17D, 21D, 23D and 25D; a later ad, with the Findlay address replacing Wellsburg, listed the same pattern numbers.

The Dalzell, Gilmore and Leighton Co. was soon established as a major glass tableware manufacturer. The firm made a wide variety of goods, ranging from common articles, such as goblets and tumblers, to fine tableware,

including some exquisite blown ware. A specialty was kerosene table lamps, and some unusual novelties were produced. Fortunately, the company advertised frequently in the trade periodicals. One of its customers was the Butler Brothers wholesale house, and their catalogues show a number of Dalzell products.

January, 1889, marked the first appearance of the new Dalzell, Gilmore and Leighton Company at the Monongahela House glass exhibit. They introduced a rather plain line called Puritan (now Kaleidoscope) in clear glass. Most pieces were engraved, and the visiting writer from *Pottery and Glassware Reporter* called them "altogether out of the usual run of pressed ware, . . . [engraved] in a masterly style."

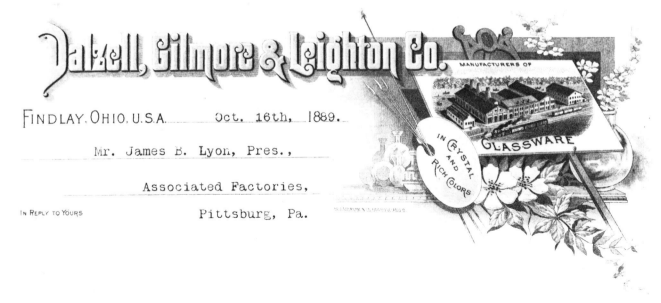

Letterhead from October, 1889.

Puritan (Kaleidoscope) engraved pitcher.

These articles are known in the Kaleidoscope pattern:
1. butter, covered
2. celery
3. plate
4. sauce
5. spooner
6. water pitcher (2 sizes)

The other lines introduced in January, 1889, were colored glass, and one of them, the celebrated Onyx glass, is probably the best-known Findlay product today. Much has been written about "Findlay Onyx," but the following discussion, based upon the glass trade periodicals of 1889, may clarify some statements in other sources. The account by *Pottery and Glassware Reporter's* writer is a good place to begin:

We want to call special attention to . . . new lines of colored ware. The first of them, which they call "Floradine" ware, is in two colors, ruby and autumn leaf, with the patterns elegantly traced on the exterior. The effect is extremely rich. In this, they make sets, bottles, jugs, celeries, molasses cans, finger bowls, sugar dusters, shaker salts and peppers, mustards, toothpicks, 4-inch nappies, 8-inch bowls, and several other articles. The other, the "Onyx" ware, is still more beautiful, and there is nothing in glass on the market to surpass it. The colors of this are onyx, bronze and ruby, and all the pieces are white-lined. Like the "Floradine," the

pattern is impressed on the exterior in graceful forms, and only for the shining surface the ware would look more like fine china than glass. Of this they now have ready creams, sugars, half-gallon jugs, molasses cans and celeries. These additions to fabrics made of glass open up a new and brilliant field to the practice of the art. The above firm have the exclusive right to make these goods, being the originators of them and they have their privileges secured by patents.

Several conclusions are clear from this account. First, the Dalzell firm saw Floradine and Onyx as separate lines, so today's collectors should not lump them together under the term Onyx. Second is the size of each line. Over a dozen Floradine articles are listed, and the Onyx line is lengthy, too. These lines constituted a substantial financial commitment, including the making of the moulds and the necessary manpower for the shops of workers.

Lastly, the columnist refers to patent rights held by the firm. This explains an announcement under the headline "Notice to Glass Manufacturers" which appeared in *Pottery and Glassware Reporter* (January 10, 1889): "You will please take notice should you be making or contemplate making Blown Ware with opalescent flowers, leaves or branches, that we have Letters Patent pending and shall defend same most rigidly should they be infringed upon. Dalzell, Gilmore and Leighton Co."

The applicable patent (U.S. Patent #402,090) was held by George W. Leighton and assigned to the firm. The specifications, however, detail the making of glass with a metallic luster (Onyx), not an opalescent effect (Floradine). Leighton may have desired to protect Floradine, for at least two Ohio Valley firms — the Buckeye Glass Company and Hobbs, Brockunier — were making similar products. Perhaps the tersely-worded "Notice to Glass Manufacturers" was part of an unsuccessful attempt to secure a patent for the Floradine line.

These items are known today in the Floradine line:
1. bowl, 8″ d.
2. butter dish
3. creamer
4. cruet w/stopper
5. pitcher
6. salt/pepper shaker
7. sauce, 4″ d.
8. spooner
9. sugar bowl, cov.
10. sugar shaker
11. syrup jug
12. toothpick
13. tumbler

The Onyx line contains these pieces:
1. bowl
2. butter dish
3. celery, tall
4. creamer
5. cruet
6. lamp
7. pickle castor

8. pitcher
9. salt/pepper shaker
10. sauce
11. spooner
12. sugar, covered
13. sugar shaker
14. syrup
15. toothpick
16. tumbler

Most Onyx items are white inside with a creamy, yellowish-white exterior, and the raised flowers and leaves are silver. Bronze flowers and leaves are seen also, and other colors have been described as "cinnamon," "rose" or "raspberry" by collectors. Onyx was advertised in a modest strip ad in *Pottery and Glassware Reporter* beginning with the January 31, 1889 issue. The ad states that Onyx was available "in various effects," and this phrase could explain the variety of colors. Some pieces are also known in amethyst glass which lack the white inner casing.

There were no ads for Onyx in *Crockery and Glass Journal,* but there is one reference to Floradine (January 31, 1889): "Among these [Dalzell products] is something entirely new, being ruby and opalescent with raised figures of flowers and leaves, producing an effect of great beauty, but which is indescribable. It is a great relief to those who have grown tired of seeing polka dots and plain knobs."

Some discussions of Onyx refer to the brittle nature of the glass and to problems encountered in making it. Don Smith interviewed members of the Dalzell family who recalled that Leighton's experiments put a financial strain on the company. On September 30, 1889, the Fostoria *Review*, quoting the *National Glass Budget*, reported that the Dalzell, Gilmore and Leighton Company had given its employees a week's notice "preparatory to closing down the whole factory." According to the story, this was necessary "because the famous oriental ware [presumably, Onyx and/or Floradine], in which they are heavily invested, is found to be as brittle as it is beautiful, and the heavy breakage makes it unprofitable for dealers . . . ." No discussion of a shutdown appeared in the Findlay newspapers.

There is other evidence concerning the financial condition of the company. Findlay banker Elijah P. Jones agreed to take a deed in trust for the Dalzell's land, buildings, and fixtures. The agreement, signed November 20, 1889, contains these terms: the glass manufacturer could borrow from Jones or the First National Bank (of which he was president) sums of money "from time to time as they might need," not to exceed $30,000 total. This arrangement freed the company from having to negotiate bank loans, and perhaps it was designed to enable the factory to meet its payroll and/or cover its drafts during a time of financial distress. The agreement was dissolved about four years later, when Jones conveyed the deed in trust back to the company.

In addition to the Onyx and Floradine wares, the Dalzell firm had yet another noteworthy item in its display. *Pottery and Glassware Reporter* (January 24, 1889) described it as ". . . a special production in the shape of a gentleman of Ethiopian descent, accoutered in elegant costume and equipped with a circumscribing brass tray containing decanter, glasses and other bacchanal accompaniments." This figural item became known as "Snowball," an incongruous name for this rather grotesque Negro representation. A "Mrs. Snowball" and two children were soon added. The Snowball figure in *Crockery and Glass Journal* (October 23, 1890) is shown with wine glasses in the Bellaire Goblet Company's Milton pattern; perhaps the Dalzell firm copied the motif or purchased the moulds.

The Dalzell, Gilmore and Leighton Company was present at the next Pittsburgh exhibition in July, 1889, but neither journal mentioned new products or pattern lines. The absence of advertising at this time may also be an indication of the company's financial problems. George W. Leighton resigned his position as "metal maker" (glass chemist and color expert) at the end of September, 1889. He retained his stock in the corporation, but his leaving may be further proof of the difficulties encountered with the Onyx ware.

During the summer of 1889, some changes were being made in the plant. The August 1, 1889, issue of *Crockery and Glass Journal* mentioned that the Dalzell's fancy colored ware was made by the tank process (as opposed to

*The only known ad for Onyx (*Pottery and Glassware Reporter*).*

79

Factory building after center furnace and stack were removed.

pot furnaces) and that the company planned to add another small tank in anticipation of the fall season. Eventually, an entire 11-pot furnace in the middle of the factory was replaced by a tank furnace. Photos of the Dalzell which show only the remaining two large chimneys were taken after this renovation.

In October, a small notice in *Pottery and Glassware Reporter* referred to kerosene lamps called Guthrie and Oklahoma made at Dalzell. As will be seen later, the production of lamps became increasingly important. In June, 1890, two more lamps, the Elite and the Corine, were shown in *Pottery and Glassware Reporter*.

The first nine months of 1890 were quiet ones, for there are few notes of company activity and little advertising in the trade journals. A major local story concerned the theft of glassware by some Dalzell employees. The *Morning Republican* reported that two men and six girls under 18 had been arrested in January, but the outcome of the cases were not revealed.

A small ad in *Pottery and Glassware Reporter* (March 17, 1890) showed a syrup jug in pattern 35D (Diagonal Block with Thumbprint—the pitcher and a miniature creamer are also known) and a blown rose bowl in a line called LaGrippe. Several months later, the trade periodical

LA GRIPPE ROSE BOWL.

Dalzell, Gilmore & Leighton Co,

FINDLAY, O.

MANUFACTURERS OF

GLASSWARE

—IN—

Crystal and Rich Colors.

35 D. SYRUP JUG.

Ad from Pottery and Glassware Reporter, March 17, 1890.

80

said that the LaGrippe pattern was "one of the best the firm ever made" and contained about 80 pieces, "one of the largest in the market." This pattern is now known as Convex Rib, and the following articles occur in clear glass:

1. bowl, 6″ d.
2. butter, covered
3. compotes, open/cov. 5″ 7″ d.
4. creamer
5. goblet
6. lamp, called "Elite" (also blue and amber)
7. rose bowl
8. sauce
9. spooner
10. sugar, covered

Convex Rib lamp.

Convex Rib covered compote.

Convex Rib spooner.

In October, 1890, the company placed full-page advertisements in the trade periodicals. The first, in *Crockery and Glass Journal* (October 23, 1890), displayed the Snowball figurals; the Old German Pipe Flask (with amber mouthpiece); and two lamp founts—Ansonia No. 43 and H. B. and H. No. 642. An ad in *Pottery and Glassware Reporter* (November 13, 1890) depicted two new decanters, the German Gentleman and the Clown. The child figure colognes were companions to the Snowball family, of course, but the Dagger cologne was a new item. Hand lamps extended the Oklahoma and Elite lines.

When the trade journal *China, Glass and Lamps* began publication on December 17, 1890, a brief news item mentioned the Snowball figurals, calling Mrs. Snowball "Daisy," and alluding to the unusual Parrot decanter. The most noteworthy information, however, concerned a new pattern, Magnolia, which was being readied for the exhibit at Pittsburgh. The Magnolia line was extensive, and articles were available in either clear glass or frosted (the frosted effect is created by exposure to hydrofluoric acid).

Dalzell, Gilmore
& Leighton Co.
FINDLAY, OHIO.

Send for Cuts and

Prices

on Novelties.

Snowball Wine Set
No. 121.

MRS. SNOWBALL DECANTER
No. 122

Ansonia Fount. No 403

Old German Pipe Flask
Amber Mouth Piece

H B & H Fount No 642

Dalzell, Gilmore
& Leighton Co.
FINDLAY, OHIO.

Send for Cuts and
Prices
on Novelties.

GERMAN GENTLEMAN DECANTER
No 124.

Clown Decanter.
No 125.

No 130 Cologne.

Dagger Cologne. No. 133.

No. 131. Cologne.

Magnolia Pattern.

"SATIN FINISH."

Magnolia ½ Gallon Tankard

Magnolia Syrup. Blown

Magnolia 9-in. Salver

Magnolia 4-in. Comport

Magnolia Butter

Magnolia Spoon

Magnolia Salt and Pepper

Magnolia Goblet

Magnolia Cream

Magnolia Sugar

Magnolia Tumbler

Magnolia 6-in Comport

Magnolia Celery

Magnolia Syrup. Pressed

Magnolia 7-in. Comport

Magnolia 8-in. Comport

Dalzell, Gilmore & Leighton Co.,
FINDLAY, OHIO.

Full page ad from Crockery and Glass Journal.

A full-page ad for Magnolia appeared in *Crockery and Glass Journal* (February 12, 1891). These items are known to today's collectors:

1. butter, covered
2. cake salver
3. celery
4. creamer
5. goblet
6. sauce, 4″ d.
7. spooner
8. sugar, covered
9. syrup jug
10. tumbler
11. water pitcher

Magnolia cake salver (clear).

Frosted Magnolia tumbler.

Over the next several months, numerous ads appeared for various Dalzell products. A display of jelly tumblers (*Crockery and Glass Journal,* February 19, 1891) ran for two months, followed by an ad for goblets (*Crockery and Glass Journal,* April 2, 1891). These jelly tumblers and goblets were common wares, the sort of staple goods made by virtually every glass tableware factory. Typically, each tumbler or goblet had an individual numerical designation. An ad for tumblers appeared in *China, Glass and Lamps,* and its writer said that Dalzell's common wares "are the handsomest assortment . . . ever brought to the attention of the trade. The shapes are elegant and they have them in many styles of ornamentation . . . ."

POTTERY AND GLASSWARE REPORTER.   5

¼ pt. 12 D. Glass Cover.   ⅓ pt. 16 D. Glass Cover.   ¼ pt. 12 D. Glass Cover.   ⅓ Qt. 16 D. Glass Cover.   ½ pt. 14 D. Glass Cover.   ½ pt. 16 D. Glass Cover.   ⅓ pt. 14 D. Glass Cover.

DALZELL, GILMORE & LEIGHTON CO.,
✦ FINDLAY, OHIO. ✦
☛ Table Glassware, Lamps, Tin Top and Glass Cover Jellies ☚

☞ *BEFORE PLACING ORDERS, WRITE FOR PRICES.* ☜

¼ pt. 10 D. Tin Top.

¼ pt. 10 D. Tin Top.

Jelly tumblers in an ad dated February 19, 1891.

3 D Goblet.
Cup Foot.   11 D Goblet.   26 D Goblet.   28 D Goblet.   20 D Goblet.   18 D Goblet.   9 D Goblet

DALZELL, + GILMORE + & + LEIGHTON + CO.

FINDLAY, OHIO.

Tableware, ✛ Lamps, ✛ Novelties.

Ad from Crockery and Glass Journal, April 2, 1891.

39 D BERRY SET.

39 D 4½-inch Berry Nappy.

39 D 9-inch Berry Bowl.

Parrot.

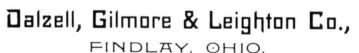

No. 1 Stamp Rack.

Dalzell, Gilmore & Leighton Co.,
FINDLAY, OHIO.
STAPLES and NOVELTIES
IN GREAT VARIETY.

Ad from China, Glass and Lamps, February 18, 1891.

Big Diamond bowl and sauce dishes.

Along with the Parrot decanter and a new article, the No. 1 Stamp Rack, a full-page ad in *China, Glass and Lamps* (February 18, 1891) displayed pattern 39D, now known as Big Diamond. These pieces occur in clear glass:

1. bowl, 9″ d.
2. butter, covered
3. cake salver
4. celery
5. compote, open, 9″ d.
6. creamer
7. pickle castor
8. sauce
9. sugar, covered
10. water pitcher

The Stamp Rack was obviously intended to hold rubber stamps in an office setting, but it resembles the pattern

Short Swirl pitcher.

S-Rib. There are similar design elements among Convex Rib (LaGrippe); S-Rib; Crystal Rib (cake salver only); Short Swirl (goblet and pitcher); Swirl and Cable; and Ring and Swirl. The latter two patterns were the most extensive of these clear glass lines. These items occur in Swirl and Cable:

1. bowls, 6″ 8″ d.
2. creamer (2 sizes)
3. honey dish
4. jelly compote
5. mug
6. pitcher, 2 sizes

S Rib cake salver.

Crystal Rib cake salver.

Swirl and Cable mug.

The following are known in Ring and Swirl:
1. bowl, 6″ d.
2. bread tray
3. butter, covered
4. cake salver
5. celery
6. creamer
7. goblet
8. relish
9. salt/pepper shaker
10. sugar, covered
11. water pitcher, 2 different bases

Ring and Swirl bowl.

By mid-1891, the firm's advertising started to change again. In the June 18, 1891 issue of *Crockery and Glass Journal,* a full-page ad displayed 23 different lamps. All were plain designs, and even their names—Captain, Elite, and Standard—were rather modest. This ad marks the beginning of the company's large scale production of kerosene lamps.

James Dalzell was in charge of the factory's exhibit at Pittsburgh in July, 1891. *China, Glass and Lamps* (July 15, 1891) mentioned lamps with ruby-colored bases; these were variations of the Standard and Captain lamps, and were called Oriole and Rubina, respectively. Some new decanters may also have been shown, for *Pottery and Glassware Reporter* (June 11, 1891) mentioned "a beautifully chiselled Highland Lassie," and *China, Glass and Lamps* noted a "bugle" decanter without providing any further description.

Another interesting, but unadvertised, figural decanter dates from late 1891. This article, which was designed by Franz Hugo Thumler of Chicago, is thought to represent boxer Bob Fitzsimmons, although the registry papers (U.S. Design #21,174) are not specific. The base of the decanter is frosted clear glass which is usually covered with black paint. The man's body is a striking opaque rosy-purplish glass. The relationship between Thumler

and the Dalzell firm is not known. The company may have purchased the rights to the design, or the decanter may have been a private mould commissioned by Thumler.

The 1892 season was the Dalzell's most ambitious to date in terms of pattern glass lines. Four new lines, each identified only by number, were listed in trade journal ads. Two lines, 45D and 49D, were described as "novel designs . . . out of the common run" (*China, Glass and Lamps,* December 31, 1891). The 43D was termed "low-priced," and the 47D was in the "moderate range." A full-page notice in *Crockery and Glass Journal* (December 31, 1891) listed a total of more than 125 items in these four different pattern lines. This extensive array of articles reflects a great financial investment in the necessary moulds, not to mention the numerous shops of workmen needed to maintain production.

Unfortunately, just one of the four patterns can be positively identified, 49D, now called Bull's Eye and Diamond Point or Reverse Torpedo. This line was well-advertised for several years, and articles are shown in Butler Brothers catalogs throughout 1892-3. On April 14, 1892, *Crockery and Glass Journal* credited Dalzell with "a phenomenal run" on pattern 49D. Earlier, *China, Glass and Lamps* (January 20, 1892) had noted the crimped pie-crust edge on salvers, baskets, etc. The following clear glass articles occur in Bull's Eye and Diamond Point; they may be engraved with various floral motifs:
1. banana dish
2. bowl
3. bride's basket
4. butter, covered

Bull's Eye and Diamond Point engraved pitcher.

CROCKERY & GLASS JOURNAL

FIXTURES · PORCELAIN · LAMPS · CLOCKS · BRONZES · DECORATIONS &c · ALSO TREATING OF

Vol. XXXV. No. 25   NEW YORK, JUNE 23, 1892. $4.00 per Annum

Acknowledged to be the Leading Lamp and Tableware Patterns.

Best Selling Lines for 1892.

49 D Spoon.

49 D Sugar.

49 D SET.

49 D Cream.

49 D Butter.

Ferdinand.

Ferdinand A. Hand.

Isabella A. Hand.

Isabella.

Ferdinand and Isabella are the King and Queen of Lamps

Four New Lines of All Glass Decorated Lamps: CASTILE, NAVARRE, ARAGON and LEON.

DALZELL, GILMORE & LEIGHTON CO.
FINDLAY, OHIO.
TABLEWARE, LAMPS, NOVELTIES.

5. cake salver
6. celery
7. compotes, open/cov, 4″ 5″ 7″ 8″ 9½″ d.
8. creamer
9. doughnut tray
10. goblet
11. lamp
12. plate
13. salt/pepper shaker
14. sauce

15. sauce, square
16. spooner
17. sugar, covered
18. tumbler
19. water pitcher, 2 sizes

Butler Brothers catalogs show Bull's Eye and Diamond Point articles together with items in Big Diamond, Convex Rib, and Swirl and Cable.

Our "IDEAL" 25-Cent Assortment.
We Have Offered Pretty Goods Before but NEVER as Beautiful as These.

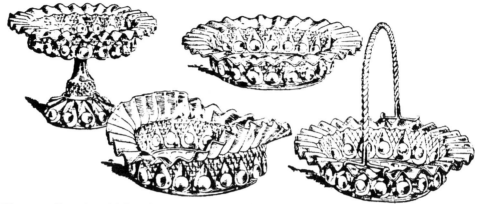

We are quite apt to think and say that each newly added assortment is just a little ahead of any other, but we are willing to leave the decision as to the merits of these 4 pieces with the customer who has confidence enough in us to buy one package on our say so. We cannot help saying here, however, that *we believe these to be the handsomest things we ever offered.*

OUR "IDEAL" ASSORTMENT OF 25-CENT CRYSTALS IS AS FOLLOWS:

½ doz. 9½-in. high-footed, scalloped, fire finished edge dishes.
½ " 11½-in. wide scalloped, fire finished edge, deep plates or dishes.
½ " 9-inch high arch metal handle dishes with scalloped fire-finished edges.
½ " 11-in. bent-in, scalloped deep dishes with fire-polished edges.

(*A total of 2 doz. to pkg. Sold only by pkg. Barrel 35c.*)   Price, $1.83 Doz.

Bulls Eye and Diamond Point items in Butler Brothers catalog, ca. 1893.

Our "BEST YET" 10-Cent Assortment.
The Latest and Most Important Addition.

As most merchants are aware, "there is glass and there is glass," but our never-failing attention to *quality* is well evidenced by this newly added assortment.

Illustrations fail to do any good ware justice, and we therefore ask for a sample package order.

THE ASSORTMENT COMPRISES 1 DOZ. EACH OF THE FOLLOWING:

8-Inch Dishes—Deep and round.
Pint Cream Pitchers.
Large Fancy Sugar Bowls and Covers.
8-Inch Oblong Dishes.
5½-Inch High Footed Bowls and Covers.
7½-Inch Fancy Crimped-Edge Dishes.

(*A total of 6 doz. to pkg. Sold only by pkg. Barrel, 35c.*)   Price, 84c Doz.

Assortment of Dalzell glass in Butler Brothers catalog, ca. 1893.

Our New Lamps For 1892

FERDINAND D.
B Collar.   Height, 10 in.

FERDINAND E.
B Collar.   Height, 10½ in.

FERDINAND C.
Either A or B Collar.
Height, 10 in.

WE ARE FILLING ORDERS NOW.

ISABELLE D.
B Collar.   Height, 10 in.

ISABELLE E.
B Collar.   Height, 10½ in.

ISABELLE C.
Either A or B Collar.
Height, 9¼ in.

*We urge the Trade to place
orders early, as our pro-
duct for this fire
has almost been
placed.*

FERDINAND O, HAND.
A Collar.   Capacity, 11 oz.

ISABELLE A, HAND.
A Collar.   Capacity, 15 oz.

THE DALZELL, GILMORE & LEIGHTON CO.
FINDLAY, OHIO.

Dalzell lamps advertised in Pottery and Glassware Reporter. December 31, 1891.

Most Original Night Lamp of the Season.

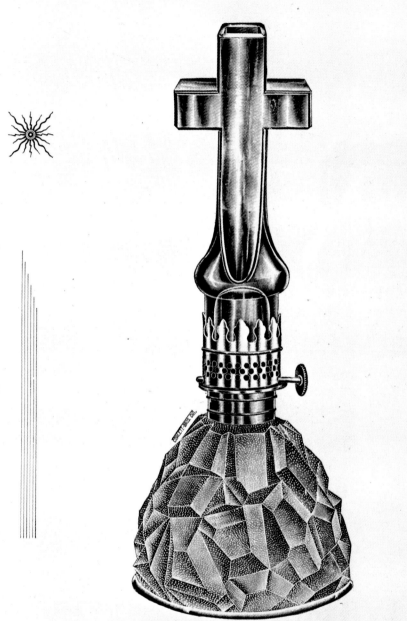

ROCK OF AGES NIGHT LAMP.

Bowl of Lamp Opal.   Chimney Crystal.   Design Patented.   Full Size Cut.

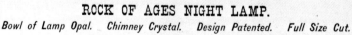

Dalzell, Gilmore & Leighton

FINDLAY, OHIO.

Rock of Ages miniature lamp.

Pottery and Glassware Reporter added an eight-page "Lamp Supplement" to its issues in mid-1892, and the Dalzell's products were prominent in the advertisements. The Ferdinand and Isabella lamps were, no doubt, named after the benefactors of Christopher Columbus, as many other glass factories were taking advantage of the publicity generated by the World's Columbian Exposition in Chicago. The Rock of Ages lamp was produced in opal (milk glass); its small base holds only a few ounces of kerosene, hence the "night light" designation.

At the time of the July, 1892, exhibition in Pittsburgh's Monongahela House, the Dalzell, Gilmore and Leighton Company was in an enviable position. *Crockery and Glass Journal* (July 20, 1892) reported that "unprecedented sales since last spring" led the firm to forego the introduction of any new patterns for the fall. Patterns such as 49D continued their strong sales, and the firm had added to its lines of lamps with some variations on the Ferdinand and Isabella: Arragon (red stem and red dots); Navarra (red stem); Leon (red stem and gold dots); and Castile (red stem). Also mentioned was a mysterious campaign flask with mirror. This may have been for the Presidential election of 1892, but there seems to be no further information about it.

When the natural gas supply began to run short in December, 1892, and the Gas Trustees ordered the glass factories to bank their furnaces, the Dalzell plant quickly prepared to convert to fuel oil. James Dalzell journeyed to Pittsburgh, and, on Christmas Eve, he sent a telegram to Findlay indicating that the newly-purchased oil-burning fixtures had been shipped. The equipment arrived on January 4, 1893, and, about a week later, the *Morning Republican* reported that "the factory [is] running at full blast with fuel oil."

In January, 1893, a new pattern, Genoese, was introduced. A reporter from *China, Glass and Lamps* visited the Monongahela House and wrote this about the Dalzell exhibit: "The new Genoese tableware pattern . . . is unquestionably the most beautiful of the many elegant lines put out by this firm and one which mere words cannot do justice to." There were no pictorial ads for this pattern, so it remains unidentified.

On February 21, 1893, James Dalzell, 39, company executive and salesman, died at the family home in Wellsburg, West Virginia. He had become ill at the Monongahela House exhibit in early February.

When the glass displays opened in July, 1893, the Dalzell firm had a new line of plain and engraved tableware with distinctive crimped edges. The crimping effect was registered by T. Steimer in February, 1893 (U.S. Design #23,495). The line was called Columbia, and full-page ads appeared in *China, Glass and Lamps* from July, 1893, until the first month of the following year. These clear glass articles, some of which may be found with engraving, are known in this popular pattern:

1. bowls, 6½″ 7½″ 8½″ d.
2. bowls, square, various sizes
3. butter, covered
4. cake salver
5. celery
6. compotes, open/cov, 5″ 7″ 8″ 9″ d.
7. creamer
8. goblet
9. sauce, square or round
10. spooner
11. sugar, covered
12. water pitcher

Columbia engraved compote.

Columbia Pattern.

OUR LATEST AND BEST.

SIXTY-TWO PIECES IN THE LINE

Dalzell, Gilmore & Leighton Co.,

FINDLAY, OHIO.

It is impossible to show the beauty of this line with cuts. Its graceful outline and newness of design is strikingly handsome.

We crimp this line in two styles in a manner never before attempted, with machines built especially for the purpose, insuring uniformity and perfection in crimping.

Our MR. C. H. LAMBIE is now at the Monongahela House, Room 156, and will be there until July 26, with full assortments of our various lines of Table Glassware and Lamps, and will be pleased to have our friends call.

Eastern Representatives: Boston, D. R Marshall, 160 Congress Street. New York, W. J. Snyder & Bro., 63 Murray Street. Philadelphia, A. S. Tomkinson, Arch Street. Baltimore, J. Beiswanger, Jr. & Co., Moore Building.

Western Representatives: San Francisco, Dieffenbacher & Wihl.

Southern Representatives: New Orleans, King & Pitcher, 54 South Peters Street.

During the fall of 1893, many glass plants had difficulties with their unionized labor forces. The companies, which had been loosely allied since 1889 as The Associated Manufacturers, wanted to eliminate the six week summer stop and, more important, to remove the restrictions on the number of items to be made (the "move") during a turn's work. The workers at Dalzell, who belonged to Local Union No. 74 of the American Flint Glass Workers Union, were steadfast in their desire to retain the restrictions. The disagreement extended through September and October, and AFGWU president W. J. Smith visited Findlay on October 30 in an attempt to end the contest. A compromise was reached in November, and the plant restarted on November 21, 1893, with over 300 workers.

The work stoppages across the country led the manufacturers to form a unified organization to deal with the AFGWU in all contract negotiations. The Associated Manufacturers, which had been formed with this intent, was not successful, largely because of a lack of support from the Ohio and Indiana plants. The new group, called the National Association of Manufacturers of Pressed and Blown Glassware, was founded in November, 1893. W. A. B. Dalzell was elected secretary, and he was an active member of the organization for many years.

In January, 1894, the Dalzell firm continued to market the Columbia line, and a new pattern, Paragon (sometimes called Kentucky), was introduced. *China, Glass and Lamps* (January 10, 1894) had a full report of the Dalzell exhibit:

> Dalzell, Gilmore and Leighton Co., of Findlay, Ohio, make a big display in their old quarters, Room 156, where C. H. Lambie is on hand to receive visitors. One of their new tableware patterns is named the "Paragon," an appellation properly descriptive of its superior excellence, and the design is entirely new and distinct from any other that has appeared in the market. There is a full line of this and the set and jugs are especially noticeable for their elegance of shape and brilliancy. . . . They have the Columbia line in both plain and decorated. Of other patterns shown here, the "Genoese" and "49D" are still standard favorites with the trade and sell very freely. There are other lines there too, and a big assortment of miscellaneous wares.

A week later, both Paragon and Columbia were advertised on the front page of *China, Glass and Lamps.* These articles occur in the Paragon pattern:

1. bowl
2. butter, covered
3. celery
4. creamer
5. dish, flared 14½" d.
6. spooner
7. sugar, covered
8. water pitcher (2 different tops)

The short Plume and Fan line in clear glass (creamer, pitcher, spooner and tumbler) may also date from this time. Plume and Fan is similar to a McKee and Brothers' pattern, Yale.

Paragon bowl (Kentucky).

Plume and Fan creamer.

Little information is available about Dalzell's products in the mid-1890s. *Pottery and Glassware Reporter* had ceased publishing, and *Crockery and Glass Journal,* which was based in New York, tended to focus upon factories in Pittsburgh and the Ohio Valley. The best coverage of glass tableware news continued to be in *China, Glass and Lamps.* The semi-annual exhibitions at the Monongahela House were dropped in favor of a three-week session held in January, so there was somewhat less news to report.

During 1894, some technological improvements were made in the Dalzell plant. One 11-pot furnace was modified to burn "producer gas" made from coal rather than the relatively expensive fuel oil. The *Morning Republican*

China Glass & Lamps

VOL. VII. NO. 6. PITTSBURGH, JANUARY 17, 1894. $2.00 PER ANNUM.

PARAGON.

Send for Prices.

Prompt Shipments.

COLUMBIA.

Our two new lines of ware, the Paragon and Columbia, are now displayed at the Monongahela House, Pittsburgh.

Dalzell, Gilmore & Leighton Co.,
FINDLAY, OHIO.

described the new systems at the Dalzell factory and the Findlay Window Glass company in its May 16, 1894, issue. Both concerns were using the principles of the Siemans regenerative furnace, in which the fuel-air mixture was preheated before combustion.

Another improvement at the Dalzell plant involved the fitting of metal lids to glass syrup jugs and collars to lamps. Traditionally, the tin tops were secured by plaster of paris. Over time, the plaster deteriorated, and the tops became loose. The collars on kerosene lamps were fitted the same way, and loose ones proved to be a substantial fire hazard. Phillip Ebeling, foreman of the mould department at the Dalzell plant, invented a machine which "clinched-on" the lids or collars by forcing them over the glass (U.S. Patent #642,307).

In January, 1895, three new patterns — Alexis, Amazon and No. 57 — were unveiled at the Monongahela House gathering. A reporter from *China, Glass and Lamps* visited the display and had this to say:

> Dalzell, Gilmore & Leighton Co. of Findlay, Ohio, changed quarters this year and now occupy room 23, where C. H. Lambie entertains callers in his customary suave manner. He has an exhibit this year of which is is especially proud, and one cannot blame him, for it is certainly attractive beyond the ordinary. In the forefront is the new "Alexis" pattern, consisting of three score and ten pieces of ware, each one of which is literally as pretty as a picture. The design is an original one, and it works out in the most brilliant ware possible to conceive, materials considered. The shallow flat dishes are unique in shape, closely following the best cut ware. Each cover is provided with a ball of crystal, so deftly put on that it is impossible to discover any mold marks. The jugs in this line are unequaled in purity and brilliancy. The mustards are wholly of glass, rendering them free from all possibility of corrosion. The individual sugars and creams are very pretty. The company is running two fine lines, the "Alexis" and No. 57, the latter plain and engraved, and a medium priced line, the "Amazon."

The Alexis pattern is known as Priscilla today. This extensive line was produced for several years, and other factories may have copied the design (the pattern was reproduced extensively in the 1950s-60s). These clear glass items are known:

1. bowl, 7½" d. (sometimes ruby flashed)
2. butter, covered
3. cake salver
4. celery
5. compote, 8½" d., scalloped edge
6. compotes, open/cov, 5" 8" d.
7. condiment tray
8. creamer
9. cruet
10. cup/saucer
11. doughnut salver
12. mug
13. rose bowl
14. salt/pepper shaker

The Beautiful "Crown Jewel" Pattern.

All in the same pattern as the tumbler.

"Crown Jewel" Wine Glass (6 doz., 34c)	36
"Crown Jewel" Sauce Dish—Fancy deep 4½-inch dish .... (6 doz. or more, 36c)	38
"Crown Jewel" Tooth-Pick Stand...... (6 doz. or more, 37c)	39
"Crown Jewel" Tumbler—Ground bottom (6 doz. or more, 40c)	42
"Crown Jewel" Cream Pitcher.......... (6 doz. or more, 40c)	42

Our "CROWN JEWEL" 50-Cent Assortment.

Heroic products of the glassmakers' art. All in the beautiful "Crown Jewel" pattern.

The assortment comprises 1-3 doz. each of the following:

8-Inch High Footed Covered Bowls
Large 2-Quart Pitchers — Very heavy.
10-Inch Square Flared Dishes—11¼ inches at corners.

1 doz. to bbl. Sold only by bbl. (Barrel 55c.)

Price, $3.35 Doz.

Our "PRIZE WINNER" 25-Cent Assortment.

Large and splendid, high-class crystal glass. All of one pattern.

The assortment comprises 1-2 doz. each of the following:

Square Deep Scalloped Dishes—9¼-inch.
High Tankard Water Pitchers.
7-In. Deep Dishes with High Covers
8¼-In. High Footed Dishes—Extra deep, scalloped.

2 doz. in pkg. Sold only by pkg (Barrel 85c.) **Price, $1.79 Doz.**

Our "CROWN JEWEL" 50-Cent Assortment.

Heroic Products of the Glassmakers' Art.

Butler Bros. 1896

These three splendid articles will not only prove magnetic attractions, but will exert such a hypnotic influence over the art-loving public as to prove themselves sellers as well.

The "Crown Jewel" Assortment Comprises 1-3 Doz. Each of the Following:

8-Inch High Footed Covered Bowls—High art article of every-day use.
Large 2-Quart Pitchers—Very heavy, very large, very beautiful.
10-Inch Square Flared Dishes—Measures 11¼ inches at corners. For fruit, etc., etc.
(Total of 1 doz. to barrel. Sold only by barrel. Barrel 35c.) Price, $3.35 Doz.

Priscilla shown in Butler Brothers catalog, ca. 1896.

15. sauce, round or square, various sizes
16. spooner
17. sugar, covered
18. toothpick
19. tumbler
20. water pitcher, two styles

In 1896, the Monongahela House exhibit attracted many buyers and manufacturers, and the sense of trade conditions was distinctly positive. The Dalzell display, unfortunately, was described only in general terms by the correspondent for *China, Glass and Lamps* (January 15, 1896):

> Mr. C. H. Lambie, room 23, is surrounded by the large, varied and brilliant products of this house, and has been booking handsome orders since his arrival. Several new lines of tableware have added to their full lines of lamps and novelties, and they are proving good sellers. Being made in the clear flint which the firm has been noted for turning out for years, their varied lines attract a far share of buyers, and few of the representatives of the jobbing trade and large distributing houses leave the exhibit without rounding out their orders with the products of this firm.

During 1896 (and the preceding year as well), the Dalzell, Gilmore and Leighton Company did not advertise specific patterns in the trade journals, so it is quite difficult to ascertain what was being made at this time.

The Ivanhoe pattern made its debut in 1897; this clear glass line was a large one, and these articles are known today:

1. butter, covered
2. cake salver
3. celery
4. cracker jar, 5¼" d.
5. creamer
6. cup
7. jelly compote
8. nappie, handled
9. plate, 10" d.
10. relish (diamond-shaped)
11. salt/pepper shaker
12. sauce, 4" d.
13. spooner
14. sugar, covered
15. syrup jug
16. toothpick
17. tumbler
18. water pitcher

In late spring, mention was made of the Dalzell's "good trade in general glassware and lamps" (*China, Glass and Lamps,* June 30, 1897), and the fall found this same journal commenting that the rush of orders to the factory marked the best sales year since 1893; a similar report appeared in the Findlay *Morning Republican* on September 6, 1897.

By late 1897, the Dalzell firm was among the nation's leading producers of kerosene lamps. A full-page ad in *Illustrated Glass and Pottery World* (November, 1897) showed lamps No. 306, 307 and 308, all of which are variations of the Crown lamps. These are known in both clear and frosted glass, and the base may be either clear or black (originally called "ebony foot"). Enamel decor may be present, also.

Ivanhoe syrup.

308. CRYSTAL SEWING LAMP.

Crown lamp as shown in Illustrated Glass and Pottery World, November, 1897.

An interesting combination of clear glass and gold stain, the now-famous Amberette pattern (which is called Klondike by many glass collectors today), was displayed at the Monongahela House in January, 1898. A plain version, called simply 75D, was available, but the writer for *China, Glass and Lamps* was clearly more interested in the decorated Amberette in his January 12, 1898, report:

C. H. Lambie, another of the old timers, looks after the interests of Dalzell, Gilmore & Leighton Co., Finlay, Ohio, in room 70. He has a brand new line called Amberette on his tables, which is probably the most original and unique in design of any shown this season. The shapes are generally square, though there are some rectangular and oval pieces, and there are narrow bands of neat small figuring crossing one another at the bottom, coming up the sides and going horizontally around each of the articles. They have this in plain crystal and also with the figured part in amber, and the effect is very striking and brilliant. They have it in transparent glass as well as satin finish and the latter presents a most pleasing appearance. There are about 50 pieces altogether. They have a new lot of jugs and several low priced lines too, but the Amberette is their leader for this season, and those who see it will agree with us in saying that it is an attractive novelty in table glass.

A full-page ad appeared in this trade journal, and a similar ad ran in *Illustrated Glass and Pottery World* for January, 1898. Most pieces are square in shape:

1. bowls, 7″ 9″
2. butter, covered
3. celery
4. condiment tray
5. creamer
6. cruet
7. cup
8. goblet
9. relish, boat-shaped
10. salt/pepper shaker
11. sauce
12. spooner
13. sugar, covered
14. toothpick
15. tumbler
16. vases, 7″ 8″ tall
17. water pitcher (also a round version)

An interesting article, called the Snyder vase by Smith, is clearly related to the Amberette line.

Salesman C. H. Lambie was quoted after the Monongahela House exhibit was over: "Things were very satisfactory with us, and business much heavier than it was last year" (*China, Glass and Lamps,* February 2, 1898). Unfortunately, there is no record of the specific patterns and/or items which contributed to the firm's success during 1898. The *Morning Republican* noted a favorable business outlook on several occasions (August 9; September 5, 1898), but the big news was the possibility that the Dalzell, Gilmore and Leighton Company would be party to a merger of glass tableware manufacturers.

The combine plan was similar to the United States Glass Company structure into which both the Columbia Glass Company and the Bellaire Goblet Company had been absorbed in 1891. Centralized management, the proponents argued, would make possible the purchase of raw materials at better prices as well as the more effective marketing of products and the general operation of the plants. A. Hart McKee of McKee and Brothers was the principal developer of the plan, and he sought to combine all the glass tableware plants in the country, including the U. S. Glass Company. The merger efforts were reported in the glass trade journals, of course, but the *Morning Republican* (November 23, 1898) said that the Dalzell firm was "strongly opposed" to the plan. By December, there was little interest in McKee's grand idea among the glass tableware manufacturers.

In January, 1899, the company displayed its wares at the Monongahela House trade show. *China, Glass and Lamps* (January 12, 1899) provided this general coverage:

The main feature of this display is an immense line of plain, figured and engraved jugs, which has become one of their specialties. In molasses cans, the firm has a fine line of samples with protruding, pressed glass lip and smooth bottoms. . . . In glass lamps, also, their clinched-on collar goods take a front rank, their lamps being made absolutely oil and air tight. . . . In general lines of glassware this firm has for years made a large variety, and their productive capacity is such that they are able to fill the largest orders promptly and regularly. Their lines are displayed in Room 70.

The mention of many different kinds of jugs suggests that the following clear glass pattern lines, otherwise impossible to pinpoint in time, may have been on the market in 1899: Concave Panels with Teardrops (pitcher);

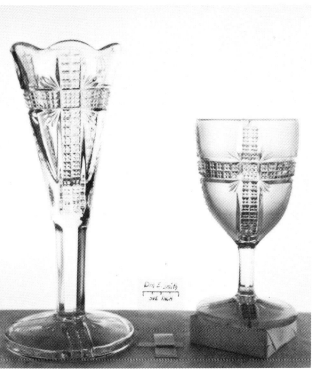

75D vase and Amberette goblet.

DALZELL, GILMORE & LEIGHTON COMPANY,

FINDLAY, OHIO.

Something entirely new and handsome, the panels are satin finished, the figured bands are stained old gold, while the deep mitres on either side are bright crystal, giving the most striking and beautiful effect of anything ever placed on the market. The line consists of 40 pieces of the most beautiful articles for table use.

AMBERETTE WARE.

Amberette Ware in crystal is known as 75 D, it is an exceptionally bright pattern, the shapes are striking and orginal.

Samples may be seen until February 5th at Room 70 Mononghela House, Pittsbnrgh, Pa.
Ask your jobber for cuts and prices.

Ad from China, Glass and Lamps, January 12, 1898.

Concave Panel with Teardrops creamer.

Teardrop tumbler.

Teardrop and Cracked Ice pitcher.

Reeding Bands (creamer and pitcher); Teardrop (butter, covered; creamer; two sizes of pitchers; spooner; sugar, covered; and tumbler); Teardrop-Clear (jelly compote, sauce and pitcher); Teardrop and Cracked Ice (butter, jelly compote, toothpick, 7″ vase and pitcher); Teardrop with Eyewinkers (cruet, jelly compote, lamp and pitcher); Thread and Lens (pitcher); and Three Birds (pitcher).

Teardrop-Clear compote.

Three Birds pitcher.

Reeding Bands creamer

Retort square bowl, crimped.

Butler Brothers catalogs from the early months of 1899 show these clear glass patterns: Beaded Drape (salt/pepper shaker and syrup jug); Beaded Fine Cut (covered butter, creamer, spooner, and covered sugar). Also depicted is the Smith pitcher, which occurs both plain (called High Plain by Heacock) and engraved, along with its companion tumbler.

The Butler Brothers catalogs also show the Retort (Owl Face) line, which is somewhat more extensive:
1. bowl, 7″ d.
2. bowl, 6″ (square)
3. celery
4. nappie, handled
5. salt dip, master
6. salt dip, individual
7. sauce, 4″ d.
8. tray, square
9. toothpick

A final pattern from the 1899 Butler Brothers catalogs is Double Fan; these articles occur in clear glass (one of the pitchers is known in green, too):
1. bowl, 6″ d.
2. butter, covered
3. celery
4. pitcher, two sizes
5. relish, rectangular
6. relish, square
7. sauce

Beaded Fine Cut creamer.

Double Fan celery.

Shortly after C. H. Lambie returned from Pittsburgh in February, 1899, the Findlay *Morning Republican* sent a reporter to interview him regarding the renewed interest in a merger plan and general business conditions:

A New York syndicate of bankers are again active in their efforts to gain control of the glass tableware factories in the United States. The Dalzell factory is one of eighteen companies named.

[Mr. Lambie] stated that he had been approached by Mr. Jameson while in Pittsburgh a few weeks ago. He informed Mr. Jameson that he could have nothing to do with the matter at this time as the Dalzell company was an incorporation.

Mr. Lambie said, however, that the gentleman would be here in a short time to look over the plant. He believed that the syndicate could secure every plant in the country if they offered a fair price. The large manufacturers, he said, were the ones who were pushing the combination scheme and the ones who needed just such a thing. In order to keep their plants in operation, they were compelled practically by competition to make some common wares at less than cost, and this fact reduced the profits on other wares.

On this account the Dalzell company does not now turn out a tumbler where it formerly turned out car load after car load. Mr. Lambie said there is a dismal outlook for some of the factories unless the combination is effected.

About a month later, rumors concerning a combination surfaced once more, but W. A. B. Dalzell was decidedly negative: "It is something like the pottery trust. Promoters are trying to fatten themselves out of a pretty scheme of combination. They have not succeeded. I hope they won't" (*Morning Republican,* March 28, 1899).

Speculation about the possible consolidation of interests was put aside in April by the news that the Dalzell plant was using a revolutionary lamp-making machine. Invented by Phillip Ebeling (U. S. Patent #653,412) and made at the local Marvin Machine Works, this device made lamps in a continuous operation, the foot pressed and the fount mould-blown from the same gather of glass. Formerly, the foot and fount were made by separate shops, and the parts fused while still hot. This procedure was certainly adequate, but glass from different pots resulted in color variations and difficulties in annealing. Ebeling's invention produced uniform ware with less breakage, but, more importantly, it reduced the need for skilled workers. The AFGWU president visited the factory in April, and an agreement was reached wherein the union accepted the use of the lamp-making machine. Within a few months, the Dalzell firm used one furnace entirely for melting batch to make lamps, and the *Morning Republican* (June 12, 1899) reported back orders for 25,000 dozen lamps!

In the summer of 1899, the glass trade publications carried more and more news of an impending merger of glass tableware interests, but C. H. Lambie told the *Morning Republican* that the Dalzell plant would not be a party to the combination. The National Glass Company, a Pennsylvania corporation, was formed in early August, 1899, by the merger of about twenty glass tableware manufacturing interests. Although the *Morning Republican* continued to insist that the Dalzell concern was "on the outside," the stockholders met in Findlay on August 24, 1899, and authorized the sale of the factory to the National Glass Company for $200,000. This meeting was apparently a well-kept secret, for when executives of the National came to Findlay, the *Morning Republican* said merely that "the object of the visit to the city could not be learned."

The story broke on October 4, 1899, when the *Morning Republican* revealed the intent of the men to induce the Dalzell firm to join the National Glass Company. The earlier stockholders' meeting, which approved the sale of the plant, is significant, however, for the other members of the National Glass Company had sold themselves to the combine for $1 and stock in the new corporation. The Dalzell's wish for a cash sale at $200,000 (and the National's willingness to meet this request) suggests that the Dalzell firm had some asset of great value or potential. Such an asset could have been the Ebeling lamp-making machine, and the National Glass Company had among its member plants two well-known lamp manufacturers, McKee and Brothers of Jeannette, Pa., and the Ohio Flint Glass Company of Lancaster, Ohio. If the National acquired the rights to Ebeling's machine, it could be used in all of the factories. In any event, the Dalzell, Gilmore and Leighton Company was sold to the National Glass Company on October 14, 1899, for $200,000.

The employees and Findlay's citizens were concerned, for they recalled that the Columbia and the Bellaire had been closed shortly after joining the United States Glass Company in the early 1890s. The *Morning Republican* was aware of speculations regarding the Dalzell plant, and a number of articles appeared which sought to allay fears that the factory would close. On December 11, 1899, W. A. B. Dalzell declared that "important improvements" were to be made at the plant, including the installation of a continuous tank furnace.

On February 8, 1900, strong winds caused both damage and injury. A wooden tower supporting a 25,000 gallon water tank collapsed onto the decorating rooms where a dozen employees were at work. Fortunately, no one was killed, but two women, Myrtle Roberts and Lucy Allesch were seriously hurt. Miss Allesch later sued the National Glass Company for $10,000, but the matter was settled out of court.

When the National Glass Company took control of the Dalzell and eighteen other plants, one of its goals was the centralization of management functions such as advertising and sales. Many travelling salesmen were let go or reassigned to other jobs, and a sample room was opened in the Heeren Building in Pittsburgh. The National did not participate in the Monongahela House exhibit in 1900, but it invited buyers to its showroom. The trade journals did not offer coverage of the lines being displayed by the National, and the company did little advertising.

In March, 1900, *China, Glass and Lamps* reported

Damage at the Dalzell plant.

that the Dalzell works was "overcrowded with orders," and that some had been passed on to other factories in the combine. Indeed, it would have been a simple matter to ship moulds to Lancaster or elsewhere. The transferring of orders may account for the fact that some Dalzell products, such as Alexis (Priscilla), were also made by other factories.

The Dalzell, Gilmore and Leighton Company made some interesting novelty articles. Except for the decanters and a few items mentioned earlier in this chapter, these novelties cannot be linked to any particular time of production. The four Euchre salts are attractive, although other concerns made similar sets. Among the most sought-after items today are two tall water pitchers, Bicycle Girl and Bringing Home the Cows. Other water pitchers are the Panelled; Branched Tree; Deer and Oak Tree; Fox and Crow; Dog and Rabbit; Heron, Racing Deer and Doe;

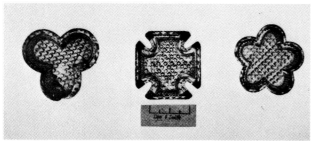

Euchre salts.

Bringing Home the Cows pitcher.

Bicycle Girl pitcher.

Fox and Crow pitcher.

Plain and Fluted, $1.30 Doz.   High Class, $1.75 Doz.

"Plain and Fluted" Pitcher Assortment—1 doz. each
of two patterns of full size pitchers, plain and fluted.
2 doz. in bbl... 1 30

Our "High Class" Pitcher Assortment—A superior
grade of goods. Large ½-gallon size, two patterns, one
plain, fluted, and one fancy as in cut. 2 doz. to pkg. 1 75

Panelled and Paragon pitchers in Butler Brothers catalog, ca. 1896.

and Squirrel. The latter three bear strong resemblances
to similar pitchers made at Greentown. All of those
pitchers were made in clear glass, but a Bicycle Girl is
also known in green. The Connecticut Skillet and the
Hairbrush were made at both Dalzell and the Indiana
Tumbler and Goblet Company, too. The little Twig mug,
known only from fragments, is similar to the Greentown
Dog and Child mug.

When the plant shut down for the summer stop on
June 15, 1900, there were rumors that it would be permanently closed. W. A. B. Dalzell denied that he was interested in moving to Chattanooga (*China, Glass and Lamps,*
August 26, 1900), and the *Morning Republican* had this
to say on November 3, 1900:

**OUR "SPECIAL
LEADER" JUG
ASSORTMENT.**

LC449—Assortment com-
prises 1 doz. each of 2 styles in
the fancy embossed rustic and
stag designs, both so-called ½-
gallon size, extra heavy, footed,
with wide tops and large handles.
Extra well made and fire polished. You can name prices
which will defy competition.
(*Total 2 doz. in bbl.
Bbl. 35c.*) Per dozen, **$1.00**

Deer and Oak Tree and Branched Tree pitchers as shown in Butler Brothers catalog, ca. 1896.

Racing Deer and Doe pitcher.

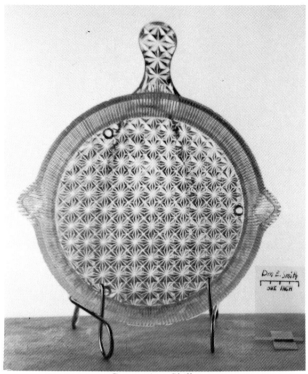

Connecticut Skillet.

Squirrel pitchers.

A statement has become current that the Dalzell glass works is slowly going out of business, and that after election, it will probably close down. This rumor was started by certain local Democratic wire-pullers, who are in need of political capital with which to influence unsuspecting voters.

"The truth is just the opposite," said the Superintendent of the Dalzell glass works yesterday. "We have had a larger business this year than for several years past. The daily orders for our goods are keeping our stock low." The firm now has 175 employees at the works. The glass workers are being paid wages fixed by the union scale.

The company has expended a large amount of money on the works this season and it is now in better condition than ever before.

"No, there is no truth in the report that we are getting ready to go out of business in this city," said the superintendent, "but we are getting ready to push the manufacture and sale of glassware more extensively this coming season."

Two days later, the newspaper featured a lengthy report on the factory, describing the various departments, and concluding that the plant was "a busy hive of industry."

By December, 1900, the National Glass Company seemed off to a successful start. The Union Trust Company of Pittsburgh accepted deeds to the National's plants as collateral for a two million dollar mortgage, and bonds paying 6% annual interest for twenty years were issued. Contracts were signed for the construction of a new plant at Cambridge, Ohio, and an expanded showroom was opened in the Heeren Building.

The National's new products for 1901 were advertised extensively in the trade periodicals. Two new pattern lines were being made at Dalzell, No. 81, Wellsburg, and No. 83, which was probably the line now known as Beaded Medallion. Wellsburg occurs in clear glass, and these pieces may also be frosted or ruby-flashed:

1. bowls, 7″ 8″ d.
2. butter, covered
3. cake salver
4. creamer
5. mug
6. punch bowl
7. punch cup
8. sauce
9. spooner
10. sugar, covered
11. syrup jug
12. toothpick
13. tumbler
14. water pitcher

Beaded Medallion pitcher and tumblers.

7. cruet
8. plate
9. sauce
10. spooner
11. sugar, covered
12. syrup jug
13. tumbler
14. water pitcher (two different bases)

Unfortunately, these two patterns are the only items traceable to Dalzell for the 1901 season, but the firm was probably making quite a variety of lamps as well, such as

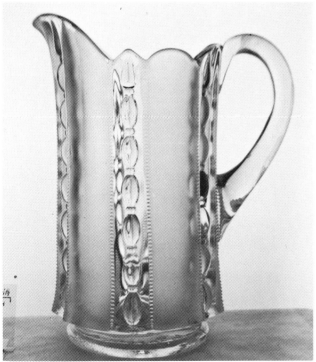

Wellsburg pitcher.

Beaded Medallion articles may be found in clear or green glass:

1. bowls, 7½″ 8½″ d.
2. butter, covered
3. cake salver
4. celery
5. compote
6. creamer

Beaded Medallion butter.

Ball Base lamp.

Sweetheart miniature lamp.

Bracket lamp.

Eyewinker Thumbprint lamp.

Two Post lamp base.

Delos covered compote.

the Ball Base lamp, the Bracket lamp, the Clark lamp, the Priscilla Star lamp, the Sweetheart lamp, and the Eye-winker Thumbprint lamp. The Two-Post lamp base may have been in production also, even though it was first made over a decade earlier.

Two other patterns date from the years during which the National Glass Company controlled the Dalzell factory. Delos was a clear glass line, available both plain and engraved, and some massive pieces were featured:

1. bowls, 6″ 7″ d.
2. bowls, square, 6″ 7″
3. cake salver
4. compotes, open/cov. 6″ 7¼″ 8½″ d.
5. rose bowl
6. pitcher
7. sauce (edge may be crimped)
8. toothpick

Only two clear glass articles are known in Diamond and Bow, the creamer and a square plate.

OUR "EXHIBITION" ASSORTMENT.

Mammoth pieces richly finished..

C295 — Brilliantly rich, almost plain pattern of purest crystal. Full finished and fire polished. *Note specially the extra large size of pieces.* Assortment comprises ¼ doz. each of the following:

¼ gal. Pitcher, stuck handle. *A 50c beauty.*
7x7 4 Corner Bowl, extra deep footed.
11 in. Extra High Cake Salver.
8½ in. High Footed Deep Bowl.

Total 2 doz. in bbl. Wt. 108 lbs. (*Bbl. 35.*)

Per dozen, **$1.87**

Diamond and Bow square plate.

Teardrop with Eyewinkers lamp.

Despite apparent success in sales, all was not well with the National, for several key executives left the combine. D. C. Jenkins, Jr., Harry Northwood and H. C. Fry resigned and sold their stock. On March 25, 1901, the Findlay *Morning Republican* reported that W. A. B. Dalzell had accepted the position of vice-president and general manager of the Fostoria Glass Company in Moundsville, West Virginia.

Calvin Roe became superintendent of the Findlay plant, and the National assured the citizens that the plant would not close. Corporate officers visited the city in April, 1901, and they were reportedly pleased with the operation there. At this time, the plant was probably producing lamps exclusively. A full-page ad in *House-furnisher* (May, 1901) showed the Dakota lamp with tripod stem and the Delaware lamp. This is the last extant ad featuring Dalzell products.

Crown lamp.

Clark lamp.

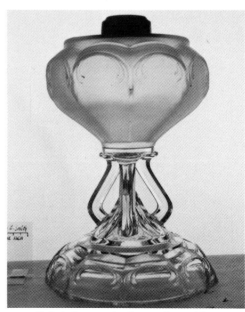

Dakota lamp, tripod stem, frosted font.

110

National Glass Co.

OPERATING
Dalzell, Gilmore & Leighton Works,
FINDLAY, OHIO.

Patent Clinch Collar Lamps, made in OO, O, A, B, C and D Stand Lamps, Flat Hand, Footed Hand, and also in C and D Sewing Lamps. Large variety of decorations, and in different patterns.

We want to call especial attention to the fact, that we are this year putting the No. 3 Collar on our largest lamps, and fitting them out with Filler, which will be especially adapted to the No. 3 burners and will not contract the wick.

Send for Price List and Illustrations.

"DAKOTA" FOOTED HAND LAMP

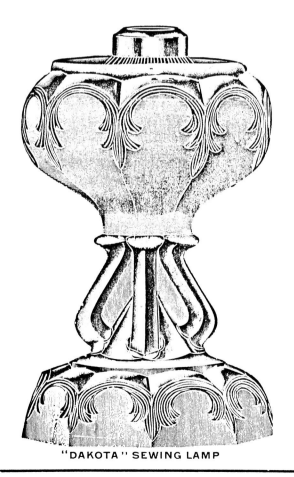

"DAKOTA" SEWING LAMP

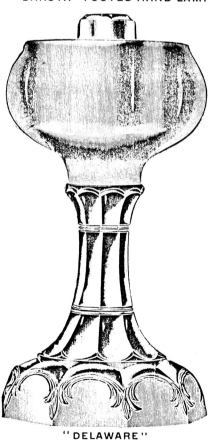

"DELAWARE"

Ad from Housefurnisher, May, 1891.

111

When Roe resigned on March 24, 1901, to join W. A. B. Dalzell at Moundsville, the possible closure of the Findlay plant must have been the chief topic of conversation in town. On Monday, May 20, 1901, the *Morning Republican* carried this long report of an interview with factory manager McClure:

Like wild fire the rumor spread over the city Saturday morning that the plant of the National Glass Company, the old Dalzell, was to be removed from Findlay. Reports so plausible, as to seem authentic, had it that the plant was to be closed at the end of the present fire, never to be started again.

The plant would be dismantled and the machinery moved to the large new plant the company is erecting at Cambridge. It was pointed out that many of the employees had left, others were leaving, that manager McClure had disposed of his property, that the company was building a fence about the plant and so on ad libitum.

Manager Horace McClure was seen at his home on Madison Avenue yesterday by a representative of the Republican and gave a stout denial to the entire story. "I have heard absolutely nothing about any such proposal," said he. "In the first place it is absurd. The rumor has been afloat for some time, but it is built upon sand. The fact that one or two of our men have gone to independent companies has aroused the rumor somewhat, but new men have been secured to take their places.

"True, I have sold my property, but I am already looking for another property further down town. We are building a fence at the plant for our own protection; it is something that should have been done years ago.

"While it is a bare possibility that the company may see fit at some future time to remove the plant from Findlay to a point nearer the coal fields, yet such a day is far distant. The large plant being built at Cambridge—it is only a third larger than ours—will be occupied next fall, most probably by some of the plants now operating in the Indiana gas belt.

"The gas there is failing rapidly; all summer, the plants at Albany, Summitville and elsewhere in Indiana have had to use wood. They will have to move or use coal shipped a great distance. That is why I should say they would be moved to Cambridge instead of the Findlay plant.

"Another thing, we have orders on our books for over forty cars of stuff that we cannot touch until next fall. We close this fire in five weeks, and will start again the first of August. It will take us until late in the fall to clear our books of the present orders.

"My instructions from the head office are to keep all the furnaces in order, the same as we have always done. This week we have put in two new pots and will put in some more before this fire is ended. If the plant were to be abandoned that

would be money wasted. The National Glass Company is quiet about its business, but it doesn't throw away money.

"While I have not been advised either way, yet I am of the opinion that there is positively nothing in the story that the Dalzell plant is to be abandoned. Everything points to its indefinite continuance."

There are 250 people on the payroll at the Dalzell factory and its removal would be a severe blow to the city. It is to be hoped that the day of such an event will be far removed. Were this city nearer the coal fields, the question would never be raised.

A subsequent article in the *Morning Republican* (June 14, 1901) took the same line, but reports in July were not as positive. When twenty men were sent to Lancaster, manager McClure denied that the plant would be closed within six months. D. E. Carle, general manager of the National, visited Findlay in August, and he also denied the persistent rumors. In late August, McClure left for Cambridge, increasing speculation that the entire work force and all fixtures were to be transferred there. The plant resumed production after the summer stop, but there are few accounts of what was being made. The Pittsburgh *Commoner and Glassworker,* a union periodical, reported ten shops making "heavy ware," probably lamps.

In late August, a Findlay shop called Noah's Ark bought all the samples at the factory and placed this notice in the *Morning Republican* (August 24, 1901):

We have purchased the entire set of glassware used by the Dalzell Glass company as samples and propose to slash the prices for a big Saturday special sale in glass.

The lot consists of 1800 pieces, embracing cake stands, cake plates, fruit bowls, pitchers, salad dishes and many other pieces.

Many of them are worth from twenty-five to fifty cents each. Today the price on each piece will be nine cents.

The sale begins sharply at 10 a.m. It hardly seems necessary to remind our customers that to secure the best pieces they should be early.

Sales may not have been up to expectations at the Noah's Ark, for a similar notice appeared in the *Morning Republican* several months later (March 15, 1902).

By late November, 1901, there seemed little doubt that the factory's days in Findlay were numbered. The *Morning Republican,* often quoting the *Commoner and Glassworker,* predicted that the plant would close about mid-January, 1902. The end came sooner, however, for "at noon, Saturday, November 30, the fires in the furnaces of the old Dalzell, Gilmore and Leighton glass factory were extinguished, never to be relighted" (*Morning Republican,* December 2, 1901).

Many workers moved quickly to jobs elsewhere, and some of the skilled hands found ready employment at the new National plant in Cambridge. Local Union No. 74 of the AFGWU was relocated to Cambridge, too. In December, the *Morning Republican* carried a number of reports detailing the dismantling of the factory. The city dug up the natural gas pipelines to the plant, and the National removed many machines and fixtures, most of which were shipped to Cambridge. The mouldmaking department, which operated its lathes with a gasoline-powered stationary engine, was the last to go, remaining until February, 1902. The *Morning Republican's* brief note concluded with a ring of sadness and finality: "This is the last crew to depart and the abandonment of the once busy plant is now complete."

In spite of the historical records available to document the Dalzell's products, a number of lines known to have been made there cannot be traced to definite points in time. Among these are several substantial pattern lines. The Six Panel Finecut line was shown in a jobber's catalog from the early 1890s:

1. bowl, 8″ d.
2. butter, covered
3. cake salver
4. celery
5. compotes, open/cov, 7″ 8″ d.
6. goblet
7. pitcher
8. salt/pepper shaker
9. syrup jug
10. tray
11. tumbler

These pieces were often decorated with an attractive flashing of dark amber applied to the small panels. Surprisingly, little of this sort of decorating seems to have been done at the Dalzell plant.

Deep File spooner and covered sugar.

The clear glass Deep File pattern (cruet, salt dip, spooner, covered sugar and 9″ vase) may have been a short line, but Starred Block was obviously extensive:

1. bowl, open/cov, 6″ 7″ 8″ d.
2. butter, covered
3. cake salver
4. celery
5. creamer
6. goblet
7. jelly compote
8. pitcher
9. sauce, various sizes
10. spooner
11. sugar, covered

Six panel Finecut goblet.

Starred Block covered compote.

Starred Block bowl and sauce dishes.

Starred Block engraved goblet.

Eyewinker compotes.

Other major lines in clear glass were Eyewinker, Hexagonal Bull's Eye, and Quaker Lady. The Eyewinker line includes these items (some of them have been reproduced in green):

    1. bowl
    2. butter, covered
    3. cake salver
    4. celery
    5. compotes, open/cov, 7″ 8″ d.
    6. creamer
    7. lamp
    8. pitcher
    9. plates, 5″ 7″ d.
   10. salt/pepper shaker
   11. sauce
   12. spooner
   13. sugar, covered

Hexagonal Bull's Eye features some very large articles:

    1. bowls, 7″ 10″ d.
    2. butter, covered
    3. celery

Eyewinker lamp.

Hexagonal Bulls Eye spooner.

Edna covered sugar bowl.

4. compotes, open/cov, 10″ d.
5. cracker jar
6. creamer
7. goblet
8. pitcher
9. spooner
10. sugar, covered

The Quaker Lady line, which is often found with fine engraving, was once mistakenly attributed to Greentown, but there is no doubt that it was a Findlay product:

1. bowls, 5″ 7″ 9″ d.
2. butter, covered
3. cake salver
4. celery
5. creamer
6. goblet
7. pitchers, several sizes
8. sauce, 4″ d.
9. spooner
10. sugar, covered

Corrigan butter dish.

Quaker Lady bowl.

The unusual Edna pattern covered candy dish has been seen in both blue and in vaseline.

Among the other clear glass pattern lines are Corrigan (covered butter; open compotes in several sizes; sauce; and wine) and Sunburst and Teepee (salt/pepper shaker; syrup jug; toothpick; and wine). A number of other patterns are known, but each occurs in a small number of articles: Concave Lens (punch cup); Dalzell Bow and Jewel (tumbler); Inverted Hobnail Arches (mug); Fantop Hobnail (8″ d. bowl, goblet and sauce); Dalzell Split Diamond (bowl and sauce); Rainey ball (cruet); Serrated Teardrop (bowl); and Star and Feather (plate). The Floral Fence plate occurs in clear, blue, amber, vaseline, opal (milk glass) and black.

Sunburst and Teepee syrup.

Fan Top Hobnail goblet.

Bow and Jewel tumbler.

Split Diamond bowl.

Inverted Hobnail Arches mug.

Serrated Teardrop bowl.

Rainey Ball cruet.

Star and Feather plate.

Floral Fence plate.

Fish Scale Swirl goblet.

117

Loganberry and Grape wine.

Clear glass goblets are the only known items in Fish-scale Swirl; Loganberry and Grape; Cherry and Fig; and Clover and Sunflower. Opal (opaque white) salt/pepper shakers occur in these patterns—Hexagonal Pyramid; Robbins; and Square Twist—and a clear shaker is known in Rhea-D.

Rhea-D salt shaker and syrup jug.

The Dalzell, Gilmore and Leighton Company was the longest-lived of Findlay's glass tableware plants, and its economic and social impacts on the city were remembered for many years. When W. A. B. Dalzell passed away in 1928, there was a lengthy obituary in the *Morning Republican* (March 15, 1928), and a similar notice appeared when C. H. Lambie passed away (October 30, 1933).

Smith engraved pitcher.

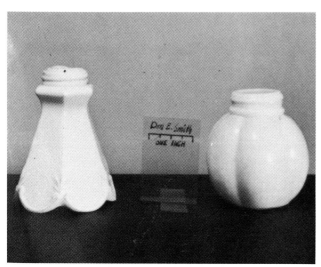

Hexagonal Pyramid shaker (left);
Robbins shaker (right)

Chapter Six
THE MODEL FLINT GLASS COMPANY

The Model Flint Glass Company was formed in the spring of 1888, and glass production began later that year. In many ways, the history of the Model firm parallels that of other glass tableware plants in Findlay, but, in other respects, the Model's story is unique.

The Findlay *Morning Republican* for April 17, 1888, was the first public mention of the arrangements for the new concern, but its report mistakenly referred to the "Novelty Flint Glass Company." The newspaper soon corrected itself, and later accounts used the Model Flint Glass Company name. The factory was located on the Dunn Place Addition, just north of the Dalzell and Bellaire Goblet plants. Most of the stockholders were Findlay men: Anderson C. Heck (president); Abraham L. Strasburger (secretary and travelling salesman); Andrew L. Stephenson (treasurer); William Parsons; J. W. Davidson; William Stephenson; Elmer Stephenson; and J. T. Leahy. Andrew Frank of Pittsburgh was also an investor. Frank Biegelow of Findlay, another stockholder, later became treasurer of the firm. The first factory manager was W. C. Walters; he was succeeded by William Russell, who came from the Dalzell firm.

Model Flint Glass Company's plant-sketches by Don Smith.

Construction began in May, 1888, and by late August the factory was nearly complete. A *Morning Republican* reporter visited the plant and wrote this engaging article on August 31, 1888:

A visit to the Model Glass Works proves it to be aptly named, and descriptive of one of the finest glass houses in the country.

The buildings have been well planned, regard being had throughout to the saving of labor, so that the ware will have to be handled as little as possible on the way from the melting pots through the presses and lears to the packers, thence to the store room, and on board the cars.

Everything is solid and substantial, with an abundance of light and ventilation, and careful attention to the comfort and health of the employees.

The handsome engine is set up and running, and the machinery, which is all new and of the best makes, is all in position. A force of skilled artisans are at work fashioning handsome designs of ware, and preparing the moulds which are to shape the products.

The furnace is nearly ready for the pots, and by the middle of September it is hoped to have the fires started.

There is no question, from the character of the men who are head of the enterprise, that the Model will meet with success. It is a home institution, some of our best business men being interested in it, and will start out most auspiciously.

Some delays were encountered in obtaining and installing machinery, and the factory began to make glass on October 2, 1888, several months later than originally planned.

The Model Flint Glass Company had its first display at the Monongahela House hotel in January, 1889. A writer for *Pottery and Glassware Reporter* (January 24, 1889) visited the Model's exhibit, and he wrote as follows:

Mr. Strasburger has charge of the samples of the Model Flint Glass Co., of Findlay, in Room 105. This company started only three months ago and have a very respectable assortment of ware for that length of time. They show two new lines of tableware in crystal, Nos. 849 and 850. The former is a full line of square block pattern, good shapes and excellent finish. No. 850 is a combination dot and square pattern and is equally well finished. They are getting out new pieces right along. They have a full line of staples, goblets, tumblers, beer mugs, etc., as well as castors, water sets, cups and saucers, inks, etc. We notice two sizes of candy trays, 7 and 8 inch, 849 pattern, and they are the nicest things of the kind going. Business is looking well with this firm and everything is going ahead. They are working on new goods and will have them ready from time to time, meanwhile their present assort-

119

ment is excellent and in every way deserving of credit.

Pattern No. 849 was probably Square Waffle; these items, all in clear glass are known: celery, 7½″ tall; goblet; pitcher; sauce dish; and tumbler. No. 850 cannot be identified for certain, but the trade journal's description suggests Diagonal Bead Bands; these clear glass articles have been found: compote, open, 10″ d.; pitcher; and wine.

Diagonal Bead Bands pitcher.

Square Waffle sauce dish.

In November, 1889, *Pottery and Glassware Reporter* mentioned that the Model was preparing two new lines for the approaching glass exhibit. One of the patterns was described as an "elegant pattern in imitation of heavy cut glass." This was probably Double Wave and Fan, introduced at the Monongahela House in January, 1890. These clear glass items occur in this pattern line:

1. bowl, 9½″ d.
2. butter, covered
3. cracker jar
4. creamer
5. creamer, miniature
6. honeydish
7. sauce, 4½″ d.
8. sugar, covered

Square Waffle goblet.

Double Wave and Fan covered butter.

The Model was also at the Monongahela House in July, 1889, but specific items in their lines were not noted by the trade journals.

Unfortunately for today's researchers, the Model did very little advertising in the trade periodicals, using a small patron ad without change for several years in two journals. One effect of such a parsimonious advertising budget was probably the scant coverage given to the Model's products in the editorial columns.

The January, 1891, exhibit at the Monongahela House was one of the largest such shows held there. *China, Glass and Lamps,* the new trade paper, provided good coverage of the various pattern lines being shown. The Model's new line was apparently "Etruscan," and a modest ad revealed that it was available plain, engraved or etched. A column in *China, Glass and Lamps* (January 14, 1891) did not mention Etruscan, but did call "Etruria" (now known as Halley's Comet) a new line. The little ads soon replaced "Etruscan" with "Etruria," so there may have been some typographical confusion. In any case, the following articles have been found in Halley's Comet; all are clear glass, and some have been decorated by engraving:

1. bowls, 7" 8" d.
2. butter, covered
3. celery
4. creamer
5. dish, rectangular
6. goblet
7. pitcher
8. sauce, 4" d.
9. spooner
10. sugar, covered
11. tray, 8" d.
12. tumbler
13. wine

Halley's Comet Wine

Pillow Encircled small pitcher.

2. butter, covered
3. cake salver
4. celery
5. compotes, open/covered, 5" 6" 7" 8" d.
6. creamer
7. lamp
8. pitcher, 2 sizes
9. sauce, 4" d.
10. spooner
11. sugar, covered
12. sugar shaker
13. tumbler
14. wine

Two other patterns, No. 857 and No. 861, were discussed as "still prime favorites," a word choice which could lead one to believe that Nos. 857 and 861 might be the patterns introduced a year earlier. No. 861 was Double Wave and Fan, of course. No. 857 is now known as Pillow Encircled, and it was an extensive line of clear glass articles, many of which have been found decorated by etching or ruby flashing:

1. bowls, 7" 8" d.

On April 22, 1891, a full-page ad showing some of the Model Flint Glass Company's products appeared in *China, Glass and Lamps.* The cut showed an interesting two-bottle castor set in the Twist pattern, but the real center of attention was the Lord's Supper bread plate, described as "the finest iron mould work ever executed." The Findlay *Morning Republican* had reported on this mould work

The Finest Iron Mold Work ever Executed.

Lord's Supper Bread Plate.

SIZE, 11x7 INCHES.

Twist Two Bottle Caster.

ENGRAVING FULL SIZE.

GLASS BASE, NICKEL-PLATED HANDLE.

SEND FOR CUTS AND PRICES TO

The Model Flint Glass Co.. Findlay Ohio.

Ad from China, Glass and Lamps, April 22, 1891.

several months earlier, in an article published November 24, 1890:

> Mr. Henry Coons, of the firm of Arduser & Co., who operate a mould factory at the West End, has just completed a mould for a glass bread plate which is as good work as has ever been done in this or any other country. It is not merely a clever copy—it is an art creation which does great credit to the artist.
>
> It represents the Lord's supper and is so suggestive and full of meaning in every situation, so true and full of expression in every last detail that it cannot be excelled.

The Arduser firm, like the Findlay Clay Pot Company, was one of those enterprises whose primary purpose was to supply fixtures and/or special tools for the various glass factories in Findlay. Such a business needs skilled machinists, and, from all reports, Henry Coons was such a man. There may have been some problems encountered in satisfactorily pressing the Lord's Supper bread plate which necessitated changes in the border design. According to *China, Glass and Lamps,* the bread plate was available both plain and etched.

The Model was present at the Monongahela House in July, 1891, and a brief account of its display appeared in *China, Glass and Lamps* on July 8, 1891. The Lord's Supper bread plate was "selling largely," and the Etruria (Halley's Comet) line contained both plain and engraved jugs and tankards. Patterns No. 857 and No. 861 were mentioned as was the Twist two-bottle set. A lamp in the Twist pattern was noted as a new addition to the line. A series of decanters in "dewdrop" (now called Hobnail) was also mentioned.

Our "JUVENILE" Glass Table Set.
A Sure 25-Cent Child-Pleaser.

A charming "make believe" table set that will please the little folks immensely. Made in a handsome pattern and elegantly finished. Comprises covered sugar bowl, covered butter dish, cream pitcher and spoon holder. Each set in box, ...Order here.   **Price, $1.69 Doz.**

Twist child's set from Butler Brothers catalog, ca. 1892-3.

Model Swirl child's creamer.

Model Swirl child's covered sugar.

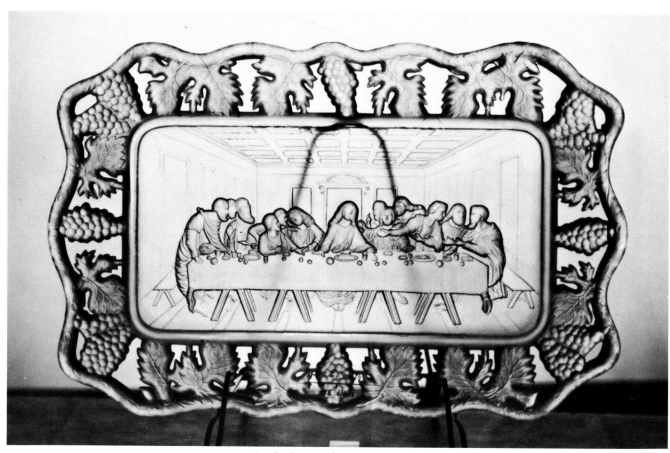

Lord's Supper plate, note open edge.

Lord's Supper plate, note closed edge.

124

Some months later, the Model began to advertise in *Crockery and Glass Journal.* In the December 3, 1891, issue, a full-page ad reiterated four patterns—Etruria, No. 849, No. 857, and No. 861—and mentioned two others, No. 851 and No. 855. The line known today as Diamond Bar and Block was No. 851, and the pattern now called Lined Ribs was No. 855. Only the cruet in clear glass has been found in Diamond Bar and Block. Clear glass goblets and wines are known in Lined Ribs, and the four-piece table set occurs in opal (opaque white).

Pottery and Glassware Reporter had the first account of the Model's next new pattern, Trump (now called Mitered Prisms) in its December 17, 1891, issue. Several months later, *Crockery and Glass Journal* reported that there were about forty pieces in the line, which it pronounced "neat, plain and low priced." None of the trade periodicals carried an illustrated ad for the pattern. In fact, the Model's small patron ad dropped from *China, Glass and Lamps* in early 1892 and did not reappear for some months. The Mitered Prisms line in clear glass was extensive:

1. bowl, 6″ d. (also with crimped rim)
2. butter, covered
3. cake salver
4. celery, 8″ tall
5. compotes, open/covered, 5″ 6″ 7½″ 8″ d.
6. cracker jar
7. creamer
8. cruet
9. cup, custard
10. goblet
11. molasses (tin top)
12. pitcher
13. salt/pepper shaker
14. sauce, 4″ d. (also with crimped rim)
15. spooner
16. sugar, covered
17. tumbler
18. wine

Diamond Bar and Block cruet.

Lined Ribs goblet.

Trump (Mitered Prisms) goblet.

Our "NEW PRIZE" 50-Cent Table Set.
"We Like It and We Feel Sure That You Will."

This takes the place of the popular Prize Set which has been sold by us for nearly two years. This is a new pattern and we expect for it even greater praise than was accorded its name sake.
....,Order here.   (*Put up 8 sets in bbl., sold only by bbl.*)   Price, 32c Set.

Trump (Mitered Prisms) table set from Butler Brothers catalog, ca. 1892-3.

In its discussion of the July, 1892, exhibit at the Monongahela House, *China, Glass and Lamps* devoted considerable attention to the Model display. A number of "new shapes in bowls and berries" had been added to the Trump line, and No. 855, Lined Ribs, seems to have become a larger line. Noted for the first time was pattern No. 837, called "a staple line consisting of table set, bowls and salvers," but, unfortunately, not described in detail. Items in the Twist pattern were displayed, including a four-piece toy set; this set is now called Model Swirl.

A significant new line in 1892 was the Gem pattern, and the reporter described a wine set in this line consisting of decanter, twelve glasses, and ten inch round tray. Today's collectors are also familiar with the mug and a miniature creamer in this pattern line. All are in clear glass.

Briefly mentioned were the Lion large lamp and the Beauty cologne bottles. A final note alluded to "special novelties" in clear glass, but gave no specifics. About a month later, in discussing the Model's "booming trade," *China, Glass and Lamps* (August 17, 1892) had this to say: "their lines have gone off like hot cakes. This is the best trade they ever had since they started...." A full-page ad in the Holiday Number of *Crockery and Glass Journal* (December 8, 1892) listed pattern Nos. 849, 851, 855, 857 and 861, all of which had been in production at least a year. Etruria and Trump were also listed, and the ad promised "an elegant new line" for 1893.

The Model Flint Glass Company's record of success in the highly-competitive glass tableware industry was threatened, to some extent, by worsening fuel problems in Findlay during December, 1892. As noted in Chapter One of this book, the Model installed an oil-fired system in January, 1893, to serve its main furnaces. All the glass factories had banked their furnaces on December 8, 1892. On November 30, the *Morning Republican* had reported that Model executives Heck and Strasburger were investigating the use of fuel oil. When the city Gas Trustees ordered the natural gas flow to the glass factories curtailed on January 12, 1893, the Model argued that they were in the midst of converting to oil. A court injunction was sought to prevent the shutoff. Judge Johnson ruled against granting an injunction to cover all of the glass factories, but he did permit the Model to draw sufficient natural gas to keep its pots warm after the January 12 shutoff. By January 20, 1893, the oil burners had been installed and all was well at the Model.

In January, 1893, a new clear glass tableware line was introduced. Named "Heck" after company president A. C. Heck, the new pattern was both brilliant and massive. *China, Glass and Lamps* had this to say: "The Heck... is a mighty bright, taking, elegant shape, and there is a full line of it. The salvers and open bowls are especially rich... This line is selling very fast already." Neither *Crockery and Glass Journal* nor *China, Glass and Lamps* carried any illustrations of the new line. These pieces are known today:

1. berry bowl
2. butter, covered
3. cake salver

Gem mug.

Heck spooner.

4. celery
5. celery tray
6. cologne bottle
7. cracker jar
8. creamer
9. cruet, two sizes
10. compotes, open/covered
11. goblet
12. jelly compote, 5" d.
13. pitcher, two sizes
14. sauce, 4" d.
15. spooner
16. sugar, covered
17. tray, 8" d.
18. tumbler
19. wine

Don Smith's fragments make possible the attribution of several other clear glass pattern lines. All seem to have been limited lines: Fine Cut Block (tumbler); Bevelled Block and Fan (cruets and sugar shaker); Coarse Cut and Block (small pitcher); Hobnail (cruet and wine); Deep Star (celery, mug, 2 sizes of pitchers and sauce); Model Bullseye (four-piece table set, cruet and pitcher); and Narrow Concave Panel (cruet). No whole pieces have been located

Bevelled Block and Fan cruet.

Fine Cut Block tumbler.

Coarse Cut and Block creamer.

Hobnail wine.

Deep Star mug.

Hobnail cruet with stopper.

Model Bullseye cruet with stopper.

128

in the following patterns: Honeycomb; Internal Diagonal Flute; Internal Prisms; Leaf and Cable (probably a lamp); Lens and Dart; Lined Rib Swirl; and Post Rib.

The Model also produced a few novelty items, although pattern glass tableware was clearly the firm's major interest. The Ivy Leaves cup and saucer occurs in amber and blue as well as clear glass. The Serpent toothpick is known in these three hues, too.

Ivy Leaves cup and saucer.

Serpent toothpick.

Perhaps the most interesting novelty item is the Russell Flower Pot. This article, a flower pot with attached saucer, was made in one operation. It was patented by the Model's manager, William F. Russell, on November 6, 1877, when he was with Hobbs, Brockunier and Company in Wheeling (U.S. Patent #196,937). Smith found fragments of the Russell Flower Pot in a deep amethyst glass (appears black at first sight).

By converting to fuel oil in early 1893, the Model avoided the fate which befell the Columbia Glass Company and the Bellaire Goblet Company. On February 3, 1893, the Findlay *Morning Republican* interviewed secretary A. L. Strasburger and reported the Model to be "running smoothly and satisfactorily . . . . Gas is used in the lehrs, but oil throughout the remainder of the factory." In late February, a meter to measure natural gas usage was installed, and, about a month later, the Model's gas bill was estimated at fifteen dollars per day. This was about half the cost of oil, and the *Morning Republican* noted the Model's concern regarding a steady supply of natural gas.

On April 3, 1893, the *Morning Republican* revealed that both the Dalzell and the Model had been approached by businessmen representing towns in Indiana or the Ohio Valley. Although the newspaper said that neither factory had "intentions of leaving the city," attractive offers were being made to induce the glass manufacturers to relocate.

One Indiana town, Albany, about 100 miles from Findlay via the Lake Erie and Western Railroad, was particularly interested in Findlay's glass plants. A gentleman named Boeckling, representing the Albany Land Company, visited the city on April 27, 1893. The next day, the *Morning Republican* revealed that the Buckeye Window Glass Company of Findlay had signed contracts pledging a move to Albany. The newspaper quoted the Albany interests to the effect that the Model would also relocate, but "the managers of that company failed to substantiate the report and it is no doubt without any foundation." On May 21, A. C. Heck and A. L. Stephenson went to Albany, and, by June 8, the *Morning Republican* was reporting that the Model would run plants in both Findlay and Albany.

After the summer stop began on July 3, 1893, the future of the Model Flint Glass Company became clear. During the rest of July, the *Morning Republican* carried brief notes regarding Model executives and other employees who were moving to new homes in Albany.

In September, 1893, this letter appeared in both *Crockery and Glass Journal* and *China, Glass and Lamps*:

> After September 23, 1893, please address all mail for us to Albany, Delaware county, Indiana, where we have removed and will be in better position than before to take care of your trade. Having our own gas wells, we will not be dependent upon any gas company for a supply of this fuel, and all orders intrusted to us will be filled with promptness and dispatch. We begin making glass at our new plant about October 1. Thanking you for your patronage in the past, and soliciting a continuation of the same, we remain,
> Very truly yours,
> The Model Flint Glass Company

The firm formed an Indiana corporation, and, on October 25, 1893, the Model Flint Glass Company of Findlay was sold to the Model Flint Glass Company of Albany, Indiana. Equipment and fixtures were shipped from Findlay to Albany. This marked the end of the Model in Findlay, of course, but it should be noted that the firm had considerable success in Indiana for the next eight years.

In late 1899, the company became part of the nineteen-member National Glass Company, as did Findlay's Dalzell, Gilmore and Leighton Company. A catalogue issued by the National about 1900 shows many Model patterns, including full lines of Heck, No. 857 (Pillow Encircled), and Trump as well as items in Etruria, Twist, Gem and Hobnail. The Lord's Supper bread plate is shown, as are the Ivy Leaves cup and saucer and the Serpent toothpick. This situation creates some difficulties for Findlay glass collectors, for it may be impossible to ascertain whether a given article was produced in Findlay or in Albany. The recent finding of the Russell Flower Pot in Chocolate glass raises this kind of problem. Since Chocolate glass was first produced by Jacob Rosenthal in late 1900 at the Indiana Tumbler and Goblet Company in Greentown, the Russell Flower Pot in that hue must date from the same general time period. Thus, the article was probably made at the Model plant in Albany, especially since the Model, like Indiana Tumbler and Goblet, was controlled by the National.

Many Model employees regarded Findlay as their real home, and the *Morning Republican* often carried news of "the Findlay colony" during the 1890s. Sometime after the National Glass Company took over the Model's operation at Albany, A. C. Heck returned to Findlay. He and his brother operated a machine shop and later formed the Buckeye Traction Ditcher Company.

Chapter Seven

THE FINDLAY FLINT GLASS COMPANY

The short history of the Findlay Flint Glass Company is both significant and tragic. The factory was small in size, but its wares were well-advertised. Just as its products were receiving great attention, the plant was destroyed by fire. The stockholders decided not to rebuild, and the Findlay Flint came to an end after less than two years of operation.

The Findlay Flint Glass Company began in late 1888 when Judge Peter Swing of Cincinnati and four Findlay men agreed to form a corporation. The president was William B. Ely, who also had an interest in the Hirsch-Ely Glass Company, a window glass plant. J. Q. Asburn of Cincinnati was vice-president. Charles W. Klein, former bookkeeper at the Columbia Glass Company, was secretary, and Elijah T. Dunn, a Findlay banker who owned the factory site, was treasurer. William McNaughton, also formerly of the Columbia, was factory manager. Judge Swing was apparently a silent investor, although he had been active as a land developer in Findlay for several years. With typical optimism, the Findlay *Morning Republican* (December 20, 1888) said that "the factory cannot fail to prove a great success in every particular."

The land was staked out on December 31, 1888, and Findlay builders Baker and McMillen began construction in late January, 1889. Newspaper reporters followed the contractor's progress closely. Cold weather was a problem, and the roof was not completed until early May. Dixon and Company of Pittsburgh installed one fifteen-pot furnace, a relatively small capacity for a glass tableware factory in the late 1880s. The "finishing touches" were being attended to in July, and the *Morning Republican,* calling the plant "mainly a home institution," said that "everyone will wish it well." Glassmaking began August 12, 1889.

Shortly after the corporation had been organized, *Pottery and Glassware Reporter* listed the officers and went on to describe the physical plant:

"[they] will have one of the best sites in Findlay, on the Heck tract, near the Heck and Tippecanoe gas wells. Part of the buildings will be 3 stories high, all brick and stone. They will be 207 feet long by 80 feet wide. The engine house will be on the east side of the buildings, but not under the same roof as the main structure, occupying 28 by 28 feet."

No photographs of the Findlay Flint are available, but an early ad in *Pottery and Glassware Reporter* features a vignette of the plant. This view is probably not accurate, for two smokestacks are present in the building on the right. A panoramic view of Findlay in 1888 depicts similar structures, and the main building has a single smokestack, as it should.

The Findlay Flint Glass Company made quite a variety of products. *Pottery and Glassware Reporter* (December 27, 1888) mentioned "all kinds of pressed and blown ware,

Original ad depicting factory.

Sketches by Don E. Smith.

note appeared: "The Findlay Flint Glass Company makes the claim that they are turning out more glassware than any other factory for the same number of pots in Northern Ohio. Exceptional good luck appears to mark the progress of this institution."

The first account of a specific line made by the Findlay Flint is in the January 16, 1890, issue of *Pottery and Glassware Reporter.* Salesman J. E. Ellis had samples on display at the Central Hotel in Pittsburgh (the Monongahela House had been damaged by fire and was under repair). The only pattern line noted was No. 9, now called Block and Double Bar. This pattern was made in clear glass only, and some articles may be found with ruby flashing. These pieces are known:

1. celery, 8½″ tall
2. compote, open, 7″ d.
3. compote, covered, 7″ d.
4. cracker jar, covered
5. creamer, miniature
6. dish, flat 4½″
7. goblet
8. tumbler
9. water pitcher, tankard, 2 styles

such as table goods, jars, lamp founts, seed cups, bird baths, and . . . novelties." An early ad in this same publication lists plain and engraved bar goods, goblets, tumblers, jelly tumblers, inks, lamps, lantern globes, and specie and French jars. The notice also solicits "private mould" work. The making of private mould glassware creates problems for the glass historian, because these products were not advertised by the factory. The owner of the mould was free to advertise the glassware, of course, but the factory which made it would usually go unmentioned. Fragments dug at the factory site may substantiate the items made there even though they were not generally advertised in catalogs or trade periodicals.

A month after glassmaking began, the Findlay Flint Glass Company was advertising in both *Pottery and Glassware Reporter* and *Crockery and Glass Journal,* but no specific pattern lines were mentioned. In the October 3, 1889, issue of *Crockery and Glass Journal,* this brief

Block and Double Bar goblet.

Block and Double Bar pitchers.

1. bell
2. bowl, 7" d.
3. butter, covered
4. cake salver
5. celery, 8" tall
6. child's table set (four pieces), without Forget-Me-Nots
7. compote, open/covered
8. creamer
9. cup/saucer
10. goblet
11. hat

Stippled Forget-Me-Not goblet.

By March, 1890, the firm was placing illustrated ads in the glass trade periodicals. An 8" Shell pattern bowl on pedestal and the Squash castor set were pictured in *Pottery and Glassware Reporter* (March 6, 1890), and the half-gallon Dot jug (Stippled Forget-Me-Not) appeared in the March 13, 1890, issue of *Crockery and Glass Journal.*

The Stippled Forget-Me-Not line was the most extensive pattern line made by the Findlay Flint. Items occur in clear glass, as well as amber, blue and opal (white milk).

Shell Bowl on Pedestal.

Stippled Forget-Me-Not covered compote.

Stippled Forget-Me-Not celery and pitcher.

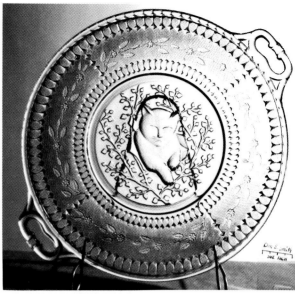

Stippled Forget-Me-Not Cat plate.

Stippled Forget-Me-Not cake salver.

Stippled Forget-Me-Not Stork plate.

12. honey dish
13. jelly compote
14. mug
15. pitcher, 2 sizes
16. plate, plain
17. plates—Baby, 7″ d., Cat, 9″ d., Stork, 11¼″ d.
18. salt/pepper shaker
19. sauce, 4″ d.
20. spooner
21. sugar, covered
22. syrup
23. toothpick
24. tumbler
25. wine

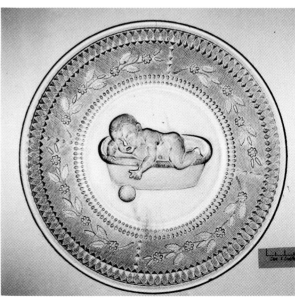

Stippled Forget-Me-Not Baby plate.

Ad from Pottery and Glassware Reporter, February 26, 1891.

In April, 1890, *Pottery and Glassware Reporter* mentioned that the Findlay Flint was making a patented inkwell with "three separate wells, a place to hold pens or pins, [and a] receptacle for sponge or pen wiper." This interesting article had been patented by Ashael P. Pichereau of Galesburg, Illinois, on March 20, 1888 (U.S. Patent #379,906) and again on December 10, 1889 (U.S. Patent #417,082). Essentially, Pichereau's patents were for a "crystal flint glass" inkwell intended for office use.

The Findlay *Morning Republican* carried an interesting report of activities at the factory on January 6, 1890; the plant was said to be making "some elegant novelties in the shape of bronzed and oxydized silver glassware, that admits of many handsome effects." *Pottery and Glassware Reporter* (February 20, 1890) mentioned a similar color development: "they are now introducing one of the most attractive features ever attempted in high art glassware. The plain ware is by a process known only to Mr. Hoare, the head of that department, made to resemble oxidized silver, and the antique in iron, old gold, copper, bronze, and brass. When finished, the figures seem brought in bas relief on a perfectly smooth surface. It is very attractive, comprises tableware and ornaments of all kinds, and is decidedly the newest thing in the high art line." One wonders if the Findlay Flint might have been producing something to rival Dalzell's Onyx line.

In June, 1890, *Pottery and Glassware Reporter* revealed that the factory was producing four lines of lamps, each containing five sizes, as well as the Pillar pattern (No. 45). One of the lamp lines was probably Beaded Chain, and another may have been Thumbprint Hex Block. The semi-annual Pittsburgh glass show, usually well-reported by the trade press, received sparse coverage in July, 1890. The show had been scaled down considerably because its usual headquarters, the Monongahela House hotel, was still undergoing repairs. Sometime during the summer of 1890, the Findlay Flint's travelling salesman, J. E. Ellis, left the firm and was replaced by R. E. Miller.

The Findlay Flint Glass Company was prominent in the glass industry periodicals during December, 1890. A new trade paper — *China, Glass and Lamps* — began publication on December 17, 1890, and the Findlay Flint had a small patron ad. Two weeks later a writer for the paper mentioned some Findlay Flint products: No. 14 ware; No. 18; and molasses cans (tin-top syrup jugs) in lines No. 16 and No. 17. A full-page ad appeared in the "Holiday Number" of *Crockery and Glass Journal* (December 11, 1890). Three items in Pillar were shown, along with the attractive Squash castor, the Shell bowl on pedestal, and a covered compote in pattern No. 9, Block and Double Bar.

Pillar creamer.

The Findlay Flint Glass Co.,

MANUFACTURERS OF

PRESSED TABLE GLASSWARE.

PLAIN AND ENGRAVED.

Also, Lamps, Jars. Beer Mugs, Bird Baths, Jellies
Novelties, etc.

FINDLAY. O.

9-INCH PILLAR BERRY.

‌ AGENTS: ‌

Dieffenbacher & Wihl, No. 318 Front St., San Francisco, Cal.
Robt. E. Young, " 187 Dearborn St., Chicago, Ill.
J. H. Bohle, " 31 Mitchel Building, St. Louis, Mo.
A. S. Tomkinson, " 532 Arch St., Philadelphia, Pa
Thos. A. O'Neill, " 140 Franklin St., Boston, Mass

R. F. MILLER, Traveling Salesman

1½ GALLON PILLAR TANKARD

7-INCH No. 9 BOWL AND COVER.

8 INCH SHELL BOWL.

SQUASH CASTOR.

PILLAR GOBLET.

Crockery and Glass Journal, December 11, 1890.

The Pillar line, called also No. 45, was a short line consisting of these articles in clear glass:

1. bowl, 9″ d.
2. butter, covered
3. celery
4. creamer
5. goblet
6. pitcher, two sizes
7. sauce, 5″ d.
8. spooner
9. sugar, covered
10. tumbler

In mid-December, 1890, *Crockery and Glass Journal* reported that the Findlay Flint had presented an engraved water set to the Farmers National Bank of Findlay, including six glasses bearing employees' names. Unfortunately, the pattern was not mentioned.

For some reason, salesman R. E. Miller did not have the Findlay Flint's wares on display at the Monongahela House until late January, 1891, several weeks after the other factories had opened their exhibits. The firm continued to advertise, however, and new ads were placed in the trade papers. The Pillar goblet and the Pichereau patent inkwell were the mainstays of these ads until April, 1891.

On April 8, 1891, the Findlay Flint Glass Company's ad was on the front page of *China, Glass and Lamps*; it

VOL. 1.   PITTSBURGH, APRIL 8, 1891.   NO. 17.

SUGAR

SPOON

＊THE＊
Findlay Flint Glass Co.,
FINDLAY, O.

No. 19 PATTERN.

CREAM

BUTTER

137

showed the four-piece table set in pattern No. 19. Another front page ad appeared in *Crockery and Glass Journal* (April 30, 1891); the tankard water pitcher was depicted, along with several other articles. In March, 1891, *China, Glass and Lamps* had reported a "big run" on pattern No. 19, and *Crockery and Glass Journal* (May 14, 1891) seems to have had this same pattern in mind: "The new shape which the Findlay Flint Glass Co. have recently put out deserves all the success that it is receiving. It is so decided a departure from the conventional patterns that it has sold on sight, and everybody speaks well of it." These clear glass items are known in pattern No. 19:

1. butter, covered
2. celery
3. creamer
4. creamer, miniature
5. goblet
6. pitchers, tankard style
7. punch cup
8. spooner
9. sugar, covered
10. tumbler

The Findlay Flint Glass Company produced several other lines, but they were limited. The following pattern lines and articles are known in clear glass: Cable Swirl; Fern (goblet); External Honeycomb (goblet and oval relish); Vertical Bar (celery and pitcher); Block with Diamond Points (tumbler); and Scalloped Edge (bowl, 7″ d., and

Cable Swirl pitcher.

Pattern No. 19 pitcher.

External Honeycomb goblet.

Fern goblet

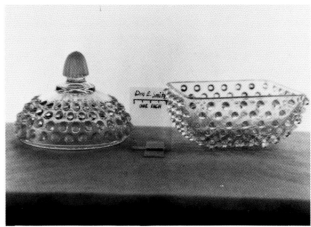

Spur Hobnail lid and square sauce.

Like many other glass factories of its time, the Findlay Flint also made "novelties," those items which are not part of any pattern line and cannot be readily classified into categories. The Pichereau inkwell is such an item, of course, and so is the teapot-shaped "Miller mustard" (Herringbone Rib), mentioned in the April 1, 1891, issue

Vertical Bar celery

Miller mustard (Herringbone Rib).

Butterfly toothpick.

sauce). Don Smith's fragments from the factory site include these additional patterns: Diamonds and Fans; Findlay Swirl; Flat Hobnail; Reed Band and Arch; and Zig-Zag. The Spur Hobnail pattern line occurs in amber and blue as well as clear glass, and these items are known.

1. creamer
2. honeydish, covered, 6″ d.
3. sauce, square
4. sugar, covered
5. tumbler

of *China, Glass and Lamps;* also reported were Daisy lamps, but no description was given. Other novelties include the Butterfly toothpick and the Drawers toothpick, both of which are known in clear glass only. The unusual Elephant Head occurs in clear, dark amber, blue and opal (opaque white).

Elephant Head.

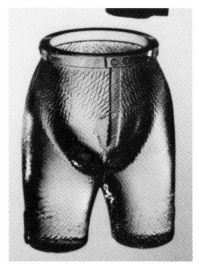

Drawers toothpick.

Some other glass items were made at the Findlay Flint Glass Company. In January, 1891, the Ohio Specialty Company transferred its operation from the Dalzell plant to the Findlay Flint; this concern marketed glass oil cans (for coal oil or kerosene) under the name "Acme Pearl."

These were quite successful in terms of sales, since much of America depended upon coal oil as fuel for heat or light. The plant also made glass discs (2⅛″ d. and ¾″ thick). These were inserted in cast iron frames and served as skylights in underground storage areas.

On May 26, 1891, the *Morning Republican* published a feature article devoted to the history and status of the Findlay Flint Glass Company. The account merits repeating in full:

The great industrial enterprises of the State of Ohio have no more important grand division than that of the manufacture of glassware. The materials for the purpose are in abundance in the neighborhood of the leading factories. Fuel is cheap and plentiful, transportation direct and economical

Acme Pearl oil cans.

while the leading manufacturers are distinguished by their enterprise and energy.

One of the leading industrial enterprises in this line in Ohio and one which has been of material advantage to the city of Findlay is the Findlay Flint Glass company. Both as regards magnitude of business conducted and superior quality of its products this concern has achieved a national reputation.

. . . The factory, a two and three story structure, 85 by 210 feet, is completely equipped throughout with all the latest modern machinery and appliances, and every possible facility is at command to secure the best possible results. Natural fuel gas, which is supplied by their own well, is used in all departments, while the most approved processes are followed.

An average force of one hundred and fifty hands are employed and the company does a business of great and growing magnitude, its products finding ready sale all over the United States and also for export trade. Quality has ever had the first consideration.

The production consists of table and bar glassware, both plain and engraved, jars, lamp and lantern globes, jelly tumblers, novelties, etc., and a ready market is found for the entire product.

The company has recently completed arrangements with the Ohio Novelty [actually, "Specialty"] Company to manufacture their Acme Pearl oil can on a royalty, and experts acknowledge that this can is now the best on the market. The factory is connected with the T. C. & S. Ry. by a side track which gives them transportation facilities and allows them to handle wares with less expense than any other plant in the city, and, taken altogether, the Findlay Flint is the best built and arranged plant in the city and it is due the officers and management to say that the great success and high development of this large and thoroughly representative establishment is in no small degree the result of their skill and energy.

The praise in the article quoted above became an irony less than two weeks later, for the Findlay Flint Glass Company was destroyed by fire late Saturday night, June 6, 1891. The *Morning Republican* reported it this way:

The origin of the fire is still a mystery. The night watchman says he discovered the fire twenty minutes before 12 o'clock, and that it had gained such headway as to have enveloped the whole north end of the building.

He turned in an alarm by telephone, but owing to the distance from the engine house, the fire was beyond control before the fire department could reach the scene. The building was a total loss, together with all the stock on hand.

. . . The total loss on the factory is about $60,000. In addition, there was on hand finished stock and raw material amounting to $15,000, all of which was destroyed. The insurance was $65,000.

. . . It is understood the factory will be rebuilt as soon as the insurance is adjusted, and it is hoped to have it completed by the commencement of the next fire, August 11th [beginning of the production season after the summer stop].

The insurance adjusters visited the site on June 16, 1891, and the debris was cleared away soon thereafter. The stockholders met on July 20, 1891, and they decided not to rebuild the factory. Over the next year or so, there were rumors that a bottle factory would be located on the site. The glassworkers and managers moved quickly to other jobs, of course, and the once highly successful Findlay Flint Glass Company became a memory.

BIBLIOGRAPHY

American Flint Glass Workers Union Archives. Toledo, Ohio (contains "Circular Letters" and all *Convention Proceedings* since 1878).

Annual Report of the Board of Gas Trustees of the City Gas Works, Findlay, Ohio, for the year ending April 1, 1890. Findlay: Courier Steam Press Printing Works, 1890.

Austin, Shirley P. "Glass Manufacture." *Twelfth Census,* Census Bulletin No. 228 (Washington, DC: government printing office, 1902).

Bannister, Lemuel. *Something About Natural Gas.* New York: American News Company, 1886.

Beardsley, D. B. *History of Hancock County, from Its Earliest Settlement to the Present Time.* Springfield: Republic Printing Co., 1881.

Bettmann, Otto. *The Good Old Days — They Were Terrible!* New York: Random House, 1974.

Bond, Marcelle. *The Beauty of Albany Glass.* Berne, IN: Publishers Printing House, 1972.

Bownocker, John Adams. *The Occurrence and Exploitation of Petroleum and Natural Gas in Ohio,* Bulletin 1 of the *Geological Survey of Ohio,* fourth series. Columbus: Ohio Geological Survey, 1903.

Brothers, J. Stanley. *Thumbnail Sketches.* Kalamazoo: by the author, 1940.

Centennial Biographical History of Hancock County Ohio. New York: Lewis Publishing Co., 1903.

China, Glass and Lamps, various issues, 1890-1903.

Connell, D. C. *Souvenir Album of Findlay, Ohio* (reprint available from the Hancock Historical Center).

Cook, Harry H. *History of the American Flint Glass Workers Union of North America, 1878-1957.* Toledo: AFGWU, 1958.

Crockery and Glass Journal, various issues, 1883-1904.

Destler, Chester McA. "The Toledo Natural Gas Pipe-Line Controversy," *The Historical Society of Northwestern Ohio Quarterly Bulletin,* 15 (April, 1943), pp. 76-110.

DiBartolomeo, Robert E. "19th Century Eastern Ohio Glass Factories," *Spinning Wheel,* October, 1971 [pp. 16-19]; November, 1971 [pp. 24-28]; and March, 1972 [pp. 22-26, 62].

Ferson, Regis and Ferson, Mary. *Yesterday's Milk Glass Today.* Pittsburgh: privately printed, 1981.

"Findlay Glass," *Western Collector,* June, 1966.

Findlay Illustrated (1889).

Glass and Pottery World, various issues, 1894-1899.

Heacock, William and Bickenheuser, Fred. *U.S. Glass from A to Z.* Marietta: Antique Publications, 1978.

Higgins, Dorcas Sours. "Lovely and Fragile Bits of Glassware Tell Days When Findlay Was Industry Center," *Republican-Courier,* June 24, 1937.

History of Hancock County, Ohio. Chicago: Warner, Beers and Co., 1886.

Hobson, G. D. and Tiratsoo, E. N. *Introduction to Petroleum Geology,* second edition. Houston: Gulf Publishing Co., 1981.

Hodkin, F. W. and Cousen, A. *A Textbook of Glass Technology.* London: Constable and Company, Ltd., 1925.

Housefurnisher: China, Glass and Pottery Review, various issues, 1898-1903.

Humphrey, William D. *Brief History of Gas and Oil in Findlay.* Findlay: 1940.

Humphrey, William D. *Findlay: The Story of a Community.* Findlay: Findlay Printing and Supply, 1961.

Hunt, John M. *Petroleum Geochemistry and Geology.* San Francisco: W. H. Freeman and Co., 1979.

Illustrated Graphic News (Cincinnati), June 18, 1887.

Innes, Lowell. *Pittsburgh Glass, 1787-1891: A History and Guide for Collectors.* Boston: Houghton Mifflin, 1976.

Kamm, Minnie Watson. *Pattern Glass Pitchers.* Vols. I-VIII. Grosse Pointe, MI: by the author, 1939-1954.

Landes, Kenneth. *Petroleum Geology of the United States.* New York: Wiley Interscience, 1970.

Light, Heat and Power, various issues, 1889-1892.

McClure, Russell S. "The Natural Gas Era in Northwestern Ohio," *The Historical Society of Northwestern Ohio Quarterly Bulletin,* 14 (July, 1942), pp. 83-105.

Measell, James. *Greentown Glass: The Indiana Tumbler and Goblet Company.* Grand Rapids: Grand Rapids Public Museum, 1979.

Measell, James. "The Western Flint and Lime Glass Protective Association, 1874-1887," *Western Pennsylvania Historical Magazine,* 66 (October, 1983), pp. 313-334.

Metz, Alice Hulett. *Early American Pattern Glass.* Columbus: by the author, 1958.

Metz, Alice Hulett. *Much More Early American Pattern Glass.* Columbus: by the author, 1965.

Mitchell, Evelyn. "Findlay Glass," *The Antiques Dealer,* March, 1969.

Mitchell, Evelyn. "Findlay's Pattern Glass," *Toledo Blade,* March 28, 1971.

National Glass Budget, various issues, 1885-1904.

Newton, J. H., Nichols, C. G., and Sprankle, A. G. *History of the Pan-Handle, West Viginia.* Wheeling: J. A. Caldwell, 1879.

New York Herald, June 11, 1887.

Orton, Edward A. *Preliminary Report on Petroleum and Inflammable Gas.* Columbus: state printer, 1886.

Orton, Edward A. *Report of the Geological Survey of Ohio,* Vol. VI, *Economic Geology.* Columbus: state printers, 1888.

Pottery and Glassware Reporter, various issues, 1879-1892.

Revi, Albert Christian. *American Pressed Glass and Figure Bottles.* New York: Thomas Nelson & Sons, 1964.

Revi, Albert Christian. *Nineteenth Century Glass: Its Genesis and Development,* revised edition. New York: Galahad Books, 1967.

Robbins, Rose Y. "The Fabulous Findlay Glass," *The Antiques Journal* (October, 1958).

Scoville, Warren C. *Revolution in Glassmaking: Entrepreneurship and Technological Change in the American Industry.* Cambridge: Harvard University Press, 1948.

Spaythe, Jacob A. *History of Hancock County, Ohio.* Toledo: B. F. Wade Printing Co., 1903.

Van Tassel, C. S. *Men of Northwestern Ohio.* Toledo: Hadley Printing Co., 1898.

Warner, Charles Dudley. "Studies of the Great West," *Harpers New Monthly Magazine,* 77 (July, 1888), pp. 267-269.

Weeks, Joseph D. "Report on the Manufacture of Glass in the United States," *Tenth Census,* Vol. II (1880).

White, Z. L. "Natural Gas in Findlay," *American Magazine,* December, 1887, pp. 199-215.

Wingerter, Charles A. *History of Greater Wheeling and Vicinity.* New York: Lewis Publishing Co., 1912.

Winter, Nevin O. *A History of Northwest Ohio.* 3 vols. Chicago: Lewis Publishing Co., 1917. 3 vols.

Index of Patterns and Items